# IRON MAN

## REPULSOR-POWER IRON MAN™
### 12" ACTION FIGURE

ELECTRONIC SPEECH!

LAUNCHING REPULSOR PROJECTILES!

REPULSOR SOUND! GLOWING REPULSORS!

BILLIONAIRE INVENTOR TONY STARK CREATES A BULLETPROOF SUIT OF IMPENETRABLE ARMOR, AND WHEN HE PUTS IT ON, HE BECOMES IRON MAN -- THE MOST POWERFUL, HIGH-TECH SUPER HERO IN THE WORLD!

MOTION-ACTIVATED SUPERSONIC FLIGHT AND COMBAT SOUNDS!

BLAST-OFF AND LANDING SOUNDS!

## YOU CAN BE IRON MAN™!

Enter the Iron Man™ sweepstakes for your chance to become an Iron Man™ action figure! To enter, and for official rules and prize details, go to **hasbro.com/ironman**

No purchase necessary. Sweepstakes ends 09/30/08. Open to legal U.S. residents. Void where prohibited.

D1228075

# IRON MAN

# BASICS

## CONTROLS

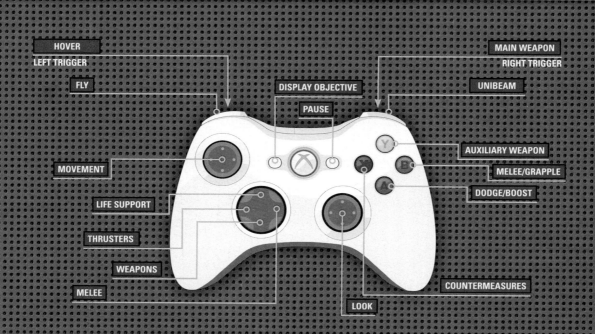

HOVER
LEFT TRIGGER
FLY
MOVEMENT
LIFE SUPPORT
THRUSTERS
WEAPONS
MELEE

DISPLAY OBJECTIVE
PAUSE
LOOK

MAIN WEAPON
RIGHT TRIGGER
UNIBEAM
AUXILIARY WEAPON
MELEE/GRAPPLE
DODGE/BOOST
COUNTERMEASURES

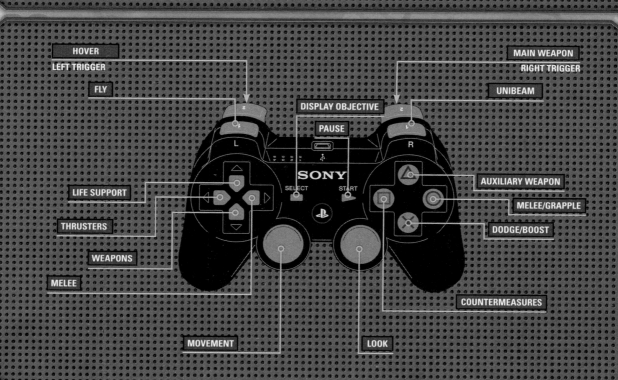

HOVER
LEFT TRIGGER
FLY
LIFE SUPPORT
THRUSTERS
WEAPONS
MELEE
MOVEMENT

DISPLAY OBJECTIVE
PAUSE
LOOK

MAIN WEAPON
RIGHT TRIGGER
UNIBEAM
AUXILIARY WEAPON
MELEE/GRAPPLE
DODGE/BOOST
COUNTERMEASURES

# GAME OVERVIEW

Iron Man is a game adaptation of the 2008 film, based upon the Marvel Comics character who originally debuted in *Tales of Suspense* #39 in March 1963. Players take on the role of Tony Stark, the brilliant but irreverent mind behind the creations of Stark Industries, the most advanced weapons technology developer on the planet. While on a routine weapons test in the Middle East, Tony was kidnapped by insurgents who demanded he build them a super-weapon. Instead, he constructs an indestructible suit of armor and uses it to escape. Realizing first-hand the devastating toll his company's weapons are inflicting on the human race, he refines the armor and uses it to perform the greatest product recall in corporate history.

As the invincible Iron Man, players must fly into enemy-controlled territories and destroy weaponry created by Stark Industries. Using Iron Man's flight capabilities and his multitude of weapons, the player must defeat some of the world's most nefarious organizations. By completing certain objectives within missions, the player earns Asset Points. Each Asset Point is worth $1 million dollars. Money earned can be spent to upgrade the Iron Man suit and improve its performance. Each upgrade costs in the range of $70 to $134 million dollars. Completing missions unlocks bonus play modes and additional Iron Man suits. By the end of the game, Tony must confront and defeat the villain behind his kidnapping and save the good name of Stark Industries.

# MODES

Iron Man is a single player game with a New Game mode, a Mission Archive mode, and One Man Army mode.

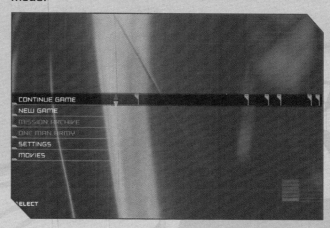

CONTINUE GAME
NEW GAME
MISSION ARCHIVE
ONE MAN ARMY
SETTINGS
MOVIES

SELECT

## NEW GAME MODE

Choose New Game from the start menu to begin the main game. Then choose a difficulty level suitable to your gaming skills: either Easy, Normal, or Formidable (Hard). The main game mode consists of a series of story-based missions the player can complete to earn Asset Points, which can be used to upgrade the Iron Man armor. Clearing missions in this mode unlocks stages in Mission Archive and One Man Army modes.

## MISSION ARCHIVE

Missions cleared in the main game mode become available for replay in the Mission Archive screen. Replaying a mission in Mission Archive mode gives the player another chance to accumulate any additional Asset Points and money not acquired previously. The player can also choose whether to don the normal Iron Man suit, or choose instead to try out other Iron Man armors unlocked by playing One Man Army mode.

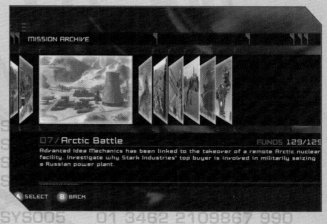

MISSION ARCHIVE

07/ Arctic Battle — FUNDS 129/129
Advanced Idea Mechanics has been linked to the takeover of a remote Arctic nuclear facility. Investigate why Stark Industries' top buyer is involved in militarily seizing a Russian power plant.

SELECT   B BACK

BASICS

ARMOR & UPGRADES

ENEMIES

MISSIONS

ONE MAN ARMY

SECRETS

## ONE MAN ARMY

One Man Army missions are unlocked by clearing certain missions in the main game mode. The objective of One Man Army mode is to eliminate 80 enemies with 10 minutes. Clearing a One Man Army mission unlocks an additional armored suit, which can be worn in Mission Archive and One Man Army modes.

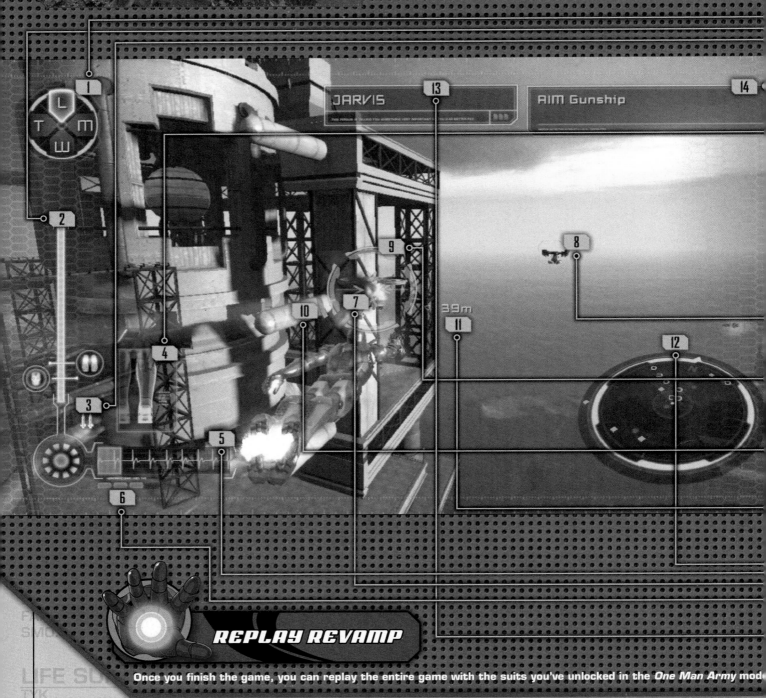

JARVIS

AIM Gunship

**REPLAY REVAMP**

Once you finish the game, you can replay the entire game with the suits you've unlocked in the *One Man Army* mode

BASICS

ARMOR & UPGRADES

ENEMIES

MISSIONS

ONE MAN ARMY

SECRETS

**1 POWER DISTRIBUTION:** Displays the key configuration for the controller's digital pad. Each direction reroutes power to a different system. The highlighted system is currently receiving power. Rerouting power displays a separate gauge that shows the action in progress. Power is fully rerouted when the progress bar disappears.

**2 ENERGY GAUGE:** Indicates Iron Man's remaining energy. Gauge empties when performing various actions. Refills over short periods of time. Lines indicate sufficient energy for using afterburners, and countermeasures.

**3 AUXILIARY WEAPON GAUGE:** Indicates when Auxiliary Weapons such as grenades or gradually forms a yellow circle around the outside of the icon while the Auxiliary Weapon is reloading.

**4 DAMAGE DIAGRAM:** Indicates point of impact where Iron Man has been struck, systems affected by damage.

**5 LIFE SUPPORT:** Indicates life support remaining. When life support is reduced to nothing, suit failure occurs.

**6 SUIT REBOOT MODULES:** The number of times remaining that the armored suit can reboot after a suit failure. When one module remains, the next system failure means game over.

**7 CROSSHAIR:** Determines the area Iron Man is facing, and where his weapons are aimed. Use the Look control to move the crosshair to the nearest target indicators in order to lock-on.

**8 TARGET INDICATOR:** Indicates the position of an enemy target. Use the Look control to move crosshair to the nearest target indicator to lock-on.

**9 LOCK-ON INDICATOR:** Indicates the primary target. Fully depress the Main Weapon button to lock-on and fire, or press the Auxiliary Weapon button to fire the selected auxiliary weapon at the locked-on target.

**10 TARGET ENERGY:** Target's remaining energy or structural integrity. Depletes as target suffers damage. When fully depleted, target is destroyed or defeated.

**11 Range Indicator:** Indicates range to the primary target. Targets at closer range suffer greater damage from Main Weapon and Unibeam fire. The maximum range for any of Iron Man's weapons is 300m.

**12 RADAR:** Indicates the compass direction faced, primary targets (orange), secondary targets (blue), optional targets (yellow) and missiles (red) in vicinity. Solid dots are ground targets, hollow circles are aircraft or airborne targets.

**13 COMMUNICATION BAR:** Indicates character currently communicating information to Iron Man.

**14 TARGET IDENTIFICATION:** Identifies the lock-on target by faction and name.

# MELEE

Press and release the Melee/Grapple button when in close range of an enemy to perform a Melee attack. Iron Man's punch is his strongest weapon, capable of destroying armored vehicles in half the time, compared to weapons. Routing power to your Melee increases the damage caused by punches. Use Melee attacks whenever possible to fight more efficiently throughout the game.

## GRAPPLE

When next to an enemy, press and hold the Melee/Grapple button to perform a Grapple. Iron Man launches into a special animation, depending on the target. For instance, when Grappling a Soldier, Iron Man yanks them off their feet and slams them face-first into the dirt. When grappling a jet-pack

donning Hover Soldier, Iron Man taps into their power system to regain life support more quickly.

When Grappling a Tank, Iron Man seizes the turret and the Melee/Grapple button icon begins flashing onscreen. Tap the Melee/Grapple button rapidly to rip the top off of the tank. You must tap the Melee/Grapple button as rapidly as the icon is flashing on the screen in order to succeed in the Grapple. Otherwise, Iron Man just gets thrown off the side of the vehicle. A Grapple attack is a great way to destroy a heavily armored vehicle immediately.

When Grappling a SAM Battery or a Howitzer, Iron Man actually takes control of the vehicle and can use it against other targets. Once you have a hold of such a vehicle, use the Look control to aim and press the Main Weapon button to fire. Grappling either vehicle type in such a manner drains its remaining energy, and the vehicle explodes when depleted.

Fighter jets can be Grappled, too! Position Iron Man so that he hovers in the flight path of a Fighter. Just before the Fighter rams Iron Man, press the Melee/Grapple button to seize hold of its wing. This is all about the timing! Iron Man shakes loose of the Fighter if you fail to press the Melee/Grapple button again when the button icon appears onscreen. Once the Fighter is under control, you can then aim the Fighter at the ground or another target, and force the Fighter to crash.

Just like catching a fighter jet, Iron Man can catch incoming missiles and actually redirect them at enemies. Once again, this is all about the timing and it may take some practice. However, once you catch the missile, you can change targets simply by turning around and getting one in sight.

### MOMENTARY CEASE FIRE

When Iron Man grapples an enemy, surrounding foes stop firing momentarily for fear of hitting their ally. Use this to your advantage, and also remember to disengage stealth or energy shields while grappling.

BASICS

ARMOR & UPGRADES

ENEMIES

MISSIONS

ONE MAN ARMY

SECRETS

**1 POWER DISTRIBUTION:** Displays the key configuration for the controller's digital pad. Each direction reroutes power to a different system. The highlighted system is currently receiving power. Rerouting power displays a separate gauge that shows the action in progress. Power is fully rerouted when the progress bar disappears.

**2 ENERGY GAUGE:** Indicates Iron Man's remaining energy. Gauge empties when performing various actions. Refills over short periods of time. Lines indicate sufficient energy for using afterburners, and countermeasures.

**3 AUXILIARY WEAPON GAUGE:** Indicates when Auxiliary Weapons such as grenades or gradually forms a yellow circle around the outside of the icon while the Auxiliary Weapon is reloading.

**4 DAMAGE DIAGRAM:** Indicates point of impact where Iron Man has been struck, systems affected by damage.

**5 LIFE SUPPORT:** Indicates life support remaining. When life support is reduced to nothing, suit failure occurs.

**6 SUIT REBOOT MODULES:** The number of times remaining that the armored suit can reboot after a suit failure. When one module remains, the next system failure means game over.

**7 CROSSHAIR:** Determines the area Iron Man is facing, and where his weapons are aimed. Use the Look control to move the crosshair to the nearest target indicators in order to lock-on.

**8 TARGET INDICATOR:** Indicates the position of an enemy target. Use the Look control to move crosshair to the nearest target indicator to lock-on.

**9 LOCK-ON INDICATOR:** Indicates the primary target. Fully depress the Main Weapon button to lock-on and fire, or press the Auxiliary Weapon button to fire the selected auxiliary weapon at the locked-on target.

**10 TARGET ENERGY:** Target's remaining energy or structural integrity. Depletes as target suffers damage. When fully depleted, target is destroyed or defeated.

**11 Range Indicator:** Indicates range to the primary target. Targets at closer range suffer greater damage from Main Weapon and Unibeam fire. The maximum range for any of Iron Man's weapons is 300m.

**12 RADAR:** Indicates the compass direction faced, primary targets (orange), secondary targets (blue), optional targets (yellow) and missiles (red) in vicinity. Solid dots are ground targets, hollow circles are aircraft or airborne targets.

**13 COMMUNICATION BAR:** Indicates character currently communicating information to Iron Man.

**14 TARGET IDENTIFICATION:** Identifies the lock-on target by faction and name.

# MOVEMENT

Use the Movement control to guide Iron Man's motion depending on the situation:

*When Iron Man is walking on the ground, use the Movement control to run in any direction.*

*When Iron Man is hovering, use the Movement control to hover left, right, forward, or backward. You can adjust Iron Man's altitude by giving more or less power to thrusters.*

*When flying, use the Movement Control to ascend, descend, or turn to the left or right.*

# LOOK

Use the Look control to alter your view of the area, and also to control the crosshairs aiming device. The crosshairs is used to target and lock-on to enemies. Iron Man fires all weapons and missiles at whatever the crosshairs point to.

# TARGETING

Available targets are marked with a small, square-like target marker, colored blue, orange, or yellow depending on the significance of the target. To lock-on to a target, move the Look control so that the crosshairs touch the target marker. The target marker changes to a large, circular lock-on marker. To lock-on to this enemy, fully depress the Main

Weapon button. Auxiliary Weapons and Iron Man's Unibeam also target the locked-on enemy.

### TARGETING TIP

Here's a tip from the pros! If you want to fire, but not lock on, hold the trigger halfway and you'll always fire at the target closest to the crosshair!

# HOVER AND ASCEND

Press the Hover button halfway when wearing the Mark II or Mark III armors (or Mark I in the Mission Archive or One Man Army modes) to hover in mid-air. Hovering is the ideal position for examining the environment, or when attacking both ground and aerial forces.

Completely depress the Hover button to ascend in altitude. Ascending makes it difficult for soldiers

and ground vehicles to attack Iron Man, and also makes attacking flying enemies easier.

Release the Hover button completely to drop to the ground. To reach the ground faster, press and hold the Fly button and use the Movement control to make Iron Man streak toward the ground.

# DODGE

While hovering and moving in any direction, press the Dodge/Boost button to dodge an oncoming attack. Dodging a missile too soon could allow the missile to redirect itself toward Iron Man. Try to hit the Dodge/Boost button only at the last second, to ensure that missiles sail harmlessly past Iron Man.

# FLIGHT

Press and hold the Fly button to fly directly ahead, in the direction Iron Man faces. While flying, use the Movement button to change course.

# BARREL-ROLL

While flying and turning left or right, press the Dodge/Boost button to perform a barrel-roll. The barrel-roll provides an exceptional method for dodging an oncoming missile, tank blast, or other attack while flying. And, it just plain *looks cool*.

# AFTERBURNERS

While flying, press and hold the Dodge/Boost button to engage Iron Man's afterburners to fly at top speed. Afterburners are great for crossing long distances quickly. Afterburners consume energy, unless power is routed to the thrusters. Certain systems and module configurations also enable Iron Man to use afterburners without consuming energy.

# GROUND POUND

Whenever Iron Man flies or falls out of the air at a great speed, he automatically performs a Ground Pound when he reaches the surface. A Ground Pound releases a tremendous impact force that inflicts severe damage to all enemies in a short range around the landing point. Use a Ground Pound to take out a squad of soldiers, or to put the finishing move on an armored vehicle.

BASICS

ARMOR & UPGRADES

ENEMIES

MISSIONS

ONE MAN ARMY

SECRETS

# MELEE

Press and release the Melee/Grapple button when in close range of an enemy to perform a Melee attack. Iron Man's punch is his strongest weapon, capable of destroying armored vehicles in half the time, compared to weapons. Routing power to your Melee increases the damage caused by punches. Use Melee attacks whenever possible to fight more efficiently throughout the game.

# GRAPPLE

When next to an enemy, press and hold the Melee/Grapple button to perform a Grapple. Iron Man launches into a special animation, depending on the target. For instance, when Grappling a Soldier, Iron Man yanks them off their feet and slams them face-first into the dirt. When grappling a jet-pack donning Hover Soldier, Iron Man taps into their power system to regain life support more quickly.

When Grappling a Tank, Iron Man seizes the turret and the Melee/Grapple button icon begins flashing onscreen. Tap the Melee/Grapple button rapidly to rip the top off of the tank. You must tap the Melee/Grapple button as rapidly as the icon is flashing on the screen in order to succeed in the Grapple. Otherwise, Iron Man just gets thrown off the side of the vehicle. A Grapple attack is a great way to destroy a heavily armored vehicle immediately.

When Grappling a SAM Battery or a Howitzer, Iron Man actually takes control of the vehicle and can use it against other targets. Once you have a hold of such a vehicle, use the Look control to aim and press the Main Weapon button to fire. Grappling either vehicle type in such a manner drains its remaining energy, and the vehicle explodes when depleted.

Fighter jets can be Grappled, too! Position Iron Man so that he hovers in the flight path of a Fighter. Just before the Fighter rams Iron Man, press the Melee/Grapple button to seize hold of its wing. This is all about the timing! Iron Man shakes loose of the Fighter if you fail to press the Melee/Grapple button again when the button icon appears onscreen. Once the Fighter is under control, you can then aim the Fighter at the ground or another target, and force the Fighter to crash.

Just like catching a fighter jet, Iron Man can catch incoming missiles and actually redirect them at enemies. Once again, this is all about the timing and it may take some practice. However, once you catch the missile, you can change targets simply by turning around and getting one in sight.

## MOMENTARY CEASE FIRE

When Iron Man grapples an enemy, surrounding foes stop firing momentarily for fear of hitting their ally. Use this to your advantage, and also remember to disengage stealth or energy shields while grappling.

# WEAPONRY

## MAIN WEAPON

Press the Main Weapon button halfway to fire the weapon built into Iron Man's gauntlets. The Main Weapon is different in each of Iron Man's suits. In the Prototype suit, Iron Man's Main Weapon is a flamethrower. In the Mark II and Mark III suit, the Main Weapon is the Repulsor system. The Repulsor fires a charged particle shot at a rate of fire and damage capability determined

by the module equipped in the system. The module equipped also determines how much energy the Repulsor uses.

Although the Main Weapon is generally Iron Man's weakest attack, it is good for taking out weak secondary targets such as mounted Flak

Turrets and Missile Turrets, soldiers, and unarmored vehicles like Fuel Trucks and Convoy Vehicles. The Main Weapon is more successful when employed in combination with the Auxiliary Weapon or Unibeam attacks. The Main Weapon can be used while on the ground, while hovering, or while flying.

## UNIBEAM

When standing on the ground or hovering, press and hold the Unibeam button to charge up a Unibeam attack. Use the Look control to aim at targets while charging. Release the Unibeam button to fire. The Unibeam is an extremely devastating attack, especially to heavy targets like tanks and boss enemies. Charging the Unibeam to its full power increases its damage and can wipe out nearly any enemy; a fully powered Unibeam strike can quickly crush even a boss! But charging up for the attack leaves Iron Man vulnerable to harm. Avoid using the Unibeam when facing overwhelming numbers of enemies or when boss enemies are

attacking. The Unibeam's power and energy consumption can be modified by equipping various system modules.

## AUXILIARY WEAPON

Press the Auxiliary Weapon to fire grenades or missiles, depending on the module equipped in the system. Auxiliary weapons fly toward the locked-on target and detonate on collision. After Auxiliary Weapons are fired, the system needs time to reload; this varies depending on the weapon. The Auxiliary Weapon Gauge displayed in the lower left corner of the screen indicates how much longer before the system is fully reloaded. A yellow circle draws around the gauge, and then disappears when the Auxiliary Weapon is ready to be fired again.

### TIME IT RIGHT!

The charging time and energy consumption of the Unibeam is different depending on which Power system module is equipped. As soon as possible, learn the timing and energy consumption pertaining to your suit configuration to avoid overcharging or depleting life support with the Unibeam.

Early on, Iron Man fires only two or three projectiles. But after upgrading the Auxiliary Weapon system Tech Level, new modules can be equipped to increase the salvo quantity to five and even seven grenades or missiles. To target multiple enemies with a single salvo, release the Main Weapon button completely and move the Look control to target several enemies while Iron Man fires grenades or missiles.

BASICS

ARMOR & UPGRADES

ENEMIES

MISSIONS

ONE MAN ARMY

SECRETS

## THINK BACKWARDS

For strategy purposes, always think of the Auxiliary Weapon as your true main weapon, and think of the Repulsor as something you just use to keep bringing the pain between salvos.

# COUNTERMEASURES

Certain upgrade modules for Iron Man's Core System enable countermeasures when equipped. Press the Countermeasures button to enable these features when energy levels permit. Press the button again to disable them. Countermeasure examples include energy shields that prevent damage from machinegun and flak fire, chaff that makes it easier to dodge homing missiles, and stealth modules that allow Iron Man to infiltrate undetected.

While countermeasures are effective, other actions drain twice as much energy as normal. For this reason, leaving countermeasures on all the time is inefficient. Countermeasures are best utilized in short periods, when enemy fire is especially heavy, and only until you can take cover or retreat to a safe distance.

## USING ENERGY SHIELDS

Boss enemies typically take short breaks between attacks. Engage energy shields while they attack, then disengage and return fire during their offensive cessation.

Also, engage shields when flying toward areas with heavy anti-air defenses. Land on the ground where most AA Turrets, Missile Turrets and SAM Batteries are ineffective, and then deactivate shields while dismantling enemy forces.

## USING CHAFF

Chaff lasts for only a short period, consumes energy, and deactivates automatically. Learn how long chaff lasts by activating it during low danger situations when fighting only a few enemies. This helps to avoid energy drain by using it too often.

Use the onscreen radar to help know when to engage chaff. When several red dots are converging on your position in the radar, engage chaff to prevent most of the missiles from striking Iron Man. Chaff is great on the Formidable difficulty.

## STEALTH COUNTERMEASURES

After activating stealth, hover or fly to a new location without dodging or using afterburners. This confuses enemies as to your location, and causes missile homing failure. Stealth becomes ineffective when weapons are fired, so sneak up behind a foe and use melee instead!

# POWER DISTRIBUTION

Press any of the buttons on the directional pad to reroute energy to any of Iron Man's four systems (clockwise from top): Life support, Melee, Weapons, and Thrusters.

### LIFE SUPPORT
Iron Man regenerates lost life at a much faster rate than normal. Always reroute to life support just after a tough battle, before headed to the next.

### MELEE
Iron Man packs a much meaner punch, inflict almost twice as much damage as normal.

### WEAPONS
All weapons systems fire and reload at a much faster rate, and inflict about one and a half times more damage than normal. They fire much faster while using approximately the same amount of energy.

### THRUSTERS
Afterburners can be used without consuming much energy, allowing Iron Man to burst on the scene fully charged and ready for battle!

# MISSION PAUSE

Press the Pause button to pause the action and open the Mission Pause menu. Options available on this menu allow you to retry the mission from the beginning, change controller, sound and video settings, or quit to the main menu to select another mode.

# SUIT CONFIGURATION

Starting with Mission 03, opportunities prior to each subsequent mission to upgrade and configure Iron Man's suit occur prior to upgrade and configure Iron Man's suit. Each of Iron Man's systems start at Tech Level 1, and can be upgraded to Tech Level 2 and then 3. Each upgrade costs tens to hundreds of millions of dollars, so achieving Hero and Bonus Objectives is very important to the upgrade process.

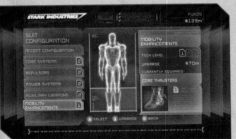

After an upgrade is purchased, new modules become available for the system. Higher level modules increase the power and capabilities of the suit. Be sure to read the description of each module to find out how. The next chapter contains a complete listing of all Iron Man's suits, upgrades and modules.

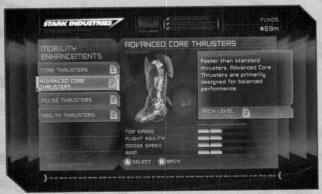

# GENERAL COMBAT TIPS

- When approaching a group of enemies, concentrate fire on relatively weak targets that do a lot of damage, including Gunships, Hover soldiers, and SAMs. Take these opponents out first to even the odds.

- Completely destroy one target before selecting a new target to reduce the damaging power of an enemy group more efficiently.

- Learn the damaging power of Iron Man's weapons, and also the resilience of your enemies. Know when an enemy is about to blow up, and target the next foe right as the killing shot is fired. This helps to avoid wasting additional time and ammunition on an enemy that is as good as dead.

- After a suit failure and system reboot, enemies do not attack for a couple of seconds. Take advantage.

- If life support is getting low, use afterburners, barrel-rolls, and chaff to escape. Find a safe place, and allow life support and energy to recharge before returning to the battle zone.

- Never let your energy empty completely. Always conserve a little to use in emergency situations as described above.

# MISSION COMPLETION AND ASSETS

When Iron Man successfully eradicates evil and saves the day, the Mission Complete screen displays. Listed on this screen are the objectives of the mission. If the objective was completed, then Asset Points are awarded. Each Asset Point represents $1,000,000 you can now spend to upgrade Iron Man's technology and systems.

- **PRIMARY OBJECTIVE:** The main objective of the mission, completed by clearing the mission. Usually yields the biggest reward obtained.

- **HERO OBJECTIVE:** An optional objective that the player has an opportunity to achieve or ignore. Assets are sometimes awarded as a whole or according to the number of times the objective was accomplished. In the Xbox 360 version, Xbox Live Achievements are unlocked for accomplishing Hero Objectives completely.

- **BONUS OBJECTIVES:** Arbitrary objectives the player can achieve by clearing the mission within a set time limit, or by destroying a specified number of enemy targets. The player can rarely achieve both during a mission. But that's what Mission Archive mode is for, right?

Press the Proceed button to continue to the next mission. If any movies or One Man Army missions are unlocked, these messages appear before moving on.

BASICS

ARMOR & UPGRADES

ENEMIES

MISSIONS

ONE MAN ARMY

SECRETS

# ARMOR SUITS AND UPGRADES

## SYSTEMS AND MODULES

By completing missions and achieving Primary Objectives, Hero Objectives, and Bonus Objectives, the player accumulates assets that can be spent to upgrade various systems of the Iron Man Mark III armor. Each upgrade becomes available to purchase when new systems modules are acquired, after completing missions. At least one or two new upgrades become available after each mission. Purchasing upgrades enables two or more modules, per upgrade.

Each module provides specific benefits, as listed in the module's description on each system's equip page. While each module provides attack and defense benefits at varying levels, some also provide special abilities, such as stealth or energy shield countermeasures. Pay close attention to each modules benefits, cons, and special abilities before equipping them prior to each subsequent mission.

| SYSTEM/TECH LEVEL | PRICE |
|---|---|
| CORE SYSTEMS 2 | $77M |
| CORE SYSTEMS 3 | $117M |
| REPULSORS 2 | $93M |
| REPULSORS 3 | $134M |
| POWER SYSTEMS 2 | $78M |
| POWER SYSTEMS 3 | $121M |
| AUXILIARY WEAPONS 2 | $82M |
| AUXILIARY WEAPONS 3 | $125M |
| MOBILITY ENHANCEMENTS 2 | $70M |
| MOBILITY ENHANCEMENTS 3 | $103M |

## Systems Upgrades

The following table indicates the assets required to purchase each Tech Level upgrade, enabling new modules to be equipped in the Iron Man suit configuration. Replay missions in Mission Archive mode to accumulate the required assets before playing harder missions.

| MISSION CLEARED | UPGRADE AVAILABLE |
|---|---|
| 02 FIRST FLIGHT | CORE SYSTEMS 2, MOBILITY ENHANCEMENTS 2 |
| 03 STARK WEAPONS | POWER SYSTEMS 2 |
| 04 MAGGIA FACTORIES | REPULSORS 2 |
| 05 MAGGIA COMPOUND | AUXILIARY WEAPONS 2 |
| 06 FLYING FORTRESS | CORE SYSTEMS 3 |
| 07 ARCTIC BATTLE | POWER SYSTEMS 3, MOBILITY ENHANCEMENTS 3 |
| 08 LOST DESTROYER | REPULSORS 3 |
| 09 ON DEFENSE | AUXILIARY WEAPONS 3 |

## Upgrade Unlocking

The table summarizes which upgrades become available after completing certain missions.

ACTIVATE LIFE SUPPORT

# Core Systems Modules

Core Systems modules improve defense and melee capabilities, and also enable countermeasure abilities that can be activated by pressing the Countermeasures button. Countermeasures consume energy when used.

BASICS

ARMOR & UPGRADES

ENEMIES

MISSIONS

ONE MAN ARMY

SECRETS

## MARK III SYSTEM

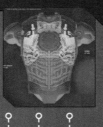

DESCRIPTION: The Mark III System offers remarkable durability without compromising mobility. This armor was constructed as a flexible foundation from which further improvements can be made.

| TECH LEVEL |
| PENETRATION RESISTANCE |
| BLAST RESISTANCE |
| MELEE |

## STRIKER SYSTEM

DESCRIPTION: Using composites and layered superconductors, the Striker System is capable of rerouting power to an energy-based shield system.

| TECH LEVEL |
| PENETRATION RESISTANCE |
| BLAST RESISTANCE |
| MELEE |

COUNTERMEASURES ENERGY SHIELD

## IMPROVED MARK III SYSTEM

DESCRIPTION: Enhanced structural integrity and the addition of anti-missile countermeasures are noteworthy additions to the Improved Mark III System.

| TECH LEVEL |
| PENETRATION RESISTANCE |
| BLAST RESISTANCE |
| MELEE |

COUNTERMEASURES CHAFF MISSILE DEFENSE

## ENERGY SHIELDS

Press the Countermeasures button to activate energy shields when any relevant module is equipped. Energy shields prevent loss of life support, consuming energy instead. If energy is deficient, the leftover amount of damage is subtracted from remaining life support. Energy shields provide a great means of avoiding system failure in emergency situations when large groups of enemies catch Iron Man off-guard. Energy Shields are incredible for closing into melee range or when you have to escape from a dire situation. To avoid letting the shields consume too much energy, press the Countermeasures button to deactivate energy shields when combat is manageable.

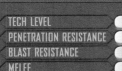

## CHAFF COUNTERMEASURES

Press the Countermeasures button when a Core System module that enables the Chaff ability is equipped to activate Chaff countermeasures. A small cloud of electromagnetic charges disperses from Iron Man's suit, causing incoming homing missiles to detonate prematurely or miss Iron Man entirely. The Chaff cloud is only effective for a few seconds, so make sure not to activate the system too early.

## ADVANCED MARK III SYSTEM

DESCRIPTION: Agile, lethal, and with significantly improved defenses, this is the most advanced version of the Mark III System available.

| TECH LEVEL |
| PENETRATION RESISTANCE |
| BLAST RESISTANCE |
| MELEE |

COUNTERMEASURES CHAFF MISSILE DEFENSE

## ADVANCED STRIKER SYSTEM

DESCRIPTION: The Advanced Striker System offers increased durability and is capable of rerouting significantly more energy to shielding systems than previous incarnations of the Striker System.

| | | | |
|---|---|---|---|
| TECH LEVEL | | | |
| PENETRATION RESISTANCE | | | |
| BLAST RESISTANCE | | | |
| MELEE | | | |

COUNTERMEASURES ENERGY SHIELD

## SPECTER SYSTEM

DESCRIPTION: The Specter System sacrifices energy to enable optical displacement countermeasures, severely disrupting hostile projectile accuracy.

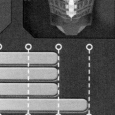

| | | | |
|---|---|---|---|
| TECH LEVEL | | | |
| PENETRATION RESISTANCE | | | |
| BLAST RESISTANCE | | | |
| MELEE | | | |

COUNTERMEASURES STEALTH

## STEALTH COUNTERMEASURES

Activating stealth enables Iron Man to take advantage of brief periods of invisibility. This causes enemies such as Soldiers, AA Turrets, and Tanks to miss when firing. However, homing missiles can still target and strike when stealth is effective.

Stealth rapidly consumes energy while active, and deactivates automatically when energy is depleted.

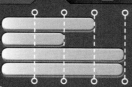

## Repulsors Modules

Repulsor system modules change the damage and rate of fire capabilities of Iron Man's Main Weapon. Higher level modules also consume greater energy, so be sure to upgrade Power Systems to a higher level prior to upgrading Repulsors. The various Ion Repulsor modules provide balanced damage and rate of fire, whereas other modules sacrifice one aspect to benefit another.

## CORE REPULSOR

DESCRIPTION: The Repulsor is a fast, accurate weapon that is equally effective against all targets.

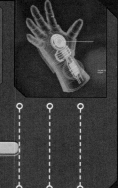

| | | | |
|---|---|---|---|
| TECH LEVEL | | | |
| DAMAGE | | | |
| RATE OF FIRE | | | |
| BLAST RADIUS | | | |
| PRECISION | | | |

## ION REPULSOR

DESCRIPTION: Ion Repulsors deliver more damage than standard Repulsors, increasing Iron Man's threat potential while maintaining a consistent rate of fire.

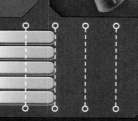

| | | | |
|---|---|---|---|
| TECH LEVEL | | | |
| DAMAGE | | | |
| RATE OF FIRE | | | |
| BLAST RADIUS | | | |
| PRECISION | | | |

## MESON REPULSOR

DESCRIPTION: Meson Repulsors offer significantly improved firepower at a slower rate of fire than standard Repulsors. This Repulsor is ideal for engaging small groups of armored targets.

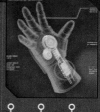

| | | | |
|---|---|---|---|
| TECH LEVEL | | | |
| DAMAGE | | | |
| RATE OF FIRE | | | |
| BLAST RADIUS | | | |
| PRECISION | | | |

BASICS

**ARMOR & UPGRADES**

ENEMIES

MISSIONS

ONE MAN ARMY

SECRETS

## GATLING REPULSOR

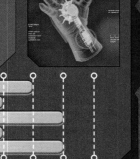

DESCRIPTION: The Gatling Repulsor system is an extremely rapid firing, light impact weapon. It is ideal for taking on lightly armored targets.

| | |
|---|---|
| TECH LEVEL | |
| DAMAGE | |
| RATE OF FIRE | |
| BLAST RADIUS | |
| PRECISION | |

## MULTI-PHASE GATLING REPULSOR

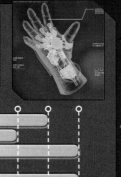

DESCRIPTION: Combining the firepower of the Ion Repulsor system with an increased rate of fire, the Multi-phase Gatling Repulsor can quickly deliver damage to numerous targets.

| | |
|---|---|
| TECH LEVEL | |
| DAMAGE | |
| RATE OF FIRE | |
| BLAST RADIUS | |
| PRECISION | |

# Power Systems Modules

Power Systems modules increase Iron Man's energy capacity, rate of regeneration, and Unibeam firepower. Certain modules can also reduce Unibeam charging time or convert damage received to energy, although life support is still diminished in spite of the conversion. Higher level power modules enable Iron Man to use weapons and afterburners for longer periods with less energy drain and faster energy regeneration.

## ADVANCED ION REPULSOR

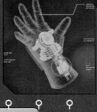

DESCRIPTION: The Advanced Ion Repulsor system enables a steady flow of accurate, high-damage fire.

| | |
|---|---|
| TECH LEVEL | |
| DAMAGE | |
| RATE OF FIRE | |
| BLAST RADIUS | |
| PRECISION | |

## PRIMARY POWER

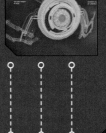

DESCRIPTION: The Primary Power system allows vast output from a compact and stable source. It requires upgrades to meet the power demands of other augmented systems.

| | |
|---|---|
| TECH LEVEL | |
| CAPACITY | |
| EFFICIENCY | |
| UNIBEAM POWER | |

## MESON CANNON REPULSOR

DESCRIPTION: The Meson Cannon Repulsor is the heaviest portable Repulsor system available. It is capable of punching through hard targets, but has a slow rate of fire.

| | |
|---|---|
| TECH LEVEL | |
| DAMAGE | |
| RATE OF FIRE | |
| BLAST RADIUS | |
| PRECISION | |

## MICRO FUSION

DESCRIPTION: The Micro Fusion power system offers improved and highly efficient power output. The additional power yield is also evident in the damage potential of the Unibeam.

| | |
|---|---|
| TECH LEVEL | |
| CAPACITY | |
| EFFICIENCY | |
| UNIBEAM POWER | |

SPECIAL RAPID UNIBEAM

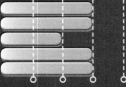

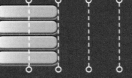

## CONVERTER AUGMENTED

DESCRIPTION: The Converter Augmented power system can convert incoming attacks into usable energy. Energy converters provide additional power under fire but do not mitigate damage.

| TECH LEVEL | | | |
| CAPACITY | | | |
| EFFICIENCY | | | |
| UNIBEAM POWER | | | |

SPECIAL **DAMAGE TO ENERGY**

## PLASMA CORE

DESCRIPTION: The Plasma Core outputs energy more efficiently than any other power plant.

| TECH LEVEL | | | |
| CAPACITY | | | |
| EFFICIENCY | | | |
| UNIBEAM POWER | | | |

SPECIAL **RAPID UNIBEAM**

## HEC AUGMENTED

DESCRIPTION: The High Efficiency Conversion power system offers improved efficiency, more power output, and an advanced collection system to convert incoming attacks into usable energy.

| TECH LEVEL | | | |
| CAPACITY | | | |
| EFFICIENCY | | | |
| UNIBEAM POWER | | | |

SPECIAL **DAMAGE TO ENERGY**

# *Auxiliary Weapons Modules*

Auxiliary Weapons modules improve the damaging power, reload time and targeting precision of the grenade/missile launcher on the backside of the gauntlets. When equipping new modules, pay attention to whether the system includes guided missiles or unguided grenades. Grenades have greater damaging power, but less range and precision. Guided missiles have less damaging power, but a virtually limitless range and excellent targeting precision.

## MICRO-GRENADES

DESCRIPTION: The Micro-Grenade dispersal system fires numerous, unguided explosives with remarkable accuracy. Grenade systems are ideal for large targets or groups of ground-based units.

| TECH LEVEL | | | |
| DAMAGE | | | |
| RATE OF FIRE | | | |
| PRECISION | | | |

SPECIAL **UNGUIDED GRENADES**

## AEGAEON MICRO-GRENADES

DESCRIPTION: The Aegaeon Micro-Grenade system is similar to the standard Micro-Grenade Dispersal System, but yields a larger and more potent grenade payload.

| TECH LEVEL | | | |
| DAMAGE | | | |
| RATE OF FIRE | | | |
| PRECISION | | | |

SPECIAL **UNGUIDED GRENADES**

## VESPID MISSILES

DESCRIPTION: Vespid Missiles are fired in volleys of three guided missiles which converge on a single target. Vespid Missiles are ideal for use against fast-moving air units.

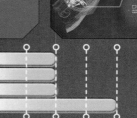

| TECH LEVEL | | | |
| DAMAGE | | | |
| RATE OF FIRE | | | |
| PRECISION | | | |

SPECIAL **GUIDED MISSILES**

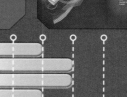
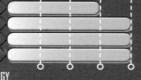

## GYGES MICRO-GRENADES

DESCRIPTION: The Gyges Micro-Grenade system fires a prolonged volley of highly explosive Micro-Grenades, effective at engaging numerous enemies simultaneously.

| TECH LEVEL | | | | |
|---|---|---|---|---|
| DAMAGE | | | | |
| RATE OF FIRE | | | | |
| PRECISION | | | | |

SPECIAL **UNGUIDED GRENADES**

## ADVANCED VESPID MISSILES

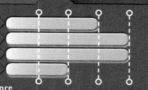

DESCRIPTION: Advanced Vespid Missiles are guided missiles carrying an improved explosive payload, fire consecutively in groups of five. This system can seek multiple targets with a single volley.

| TECH LEVEL | | | | |
|---|---|---|---|---|
| DAMAGE | | | | |
| RATE OF FIRE | | | | |
| PRECISION | | | | |

SPECIAL **GUIDED MISSILES**

## *Mobility Enhancements Modules*

Mobility enhancements modify Iron Man's flight speed, maneuverability, and the damaging power of ramming into a target. Higher level modules consume greater amounts of energy. Therefore, it is wise to upgrade and equip higher level power systems prior to upgrading higher level thruster modules.

## CORE THRUSTERS

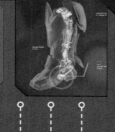

DESCRIPTION: The Core Thruster system allows for high-speed flight, maneuverability and stable hovering. These thrusters serve as a platform for further advances in speed, efficiency and maneuverability.

| TECH LEVEL | | | | |
|---|---|---|---|---|
| TOP SPEED | | | | |
| FLIGHT AGILITY | | | | |
| DODGE SPEED | | | | |
| RAM | | | | |

## ADVANCED CORE THRUSTERS

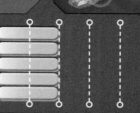

DESCRIPTION: Faster than standard thrusters, Advanced Core Thrusters are primarily designed for balanced performance.

| TECH LEVEL | | | | |
|---|---|---|---|---|
| TOP SPEED | | | | |
| FLIGHT AGILITY | | | | |
| DODGE SPEED | | | | |
| RAM | | | | |

## PULSE THRUSTERS

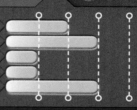

DESCRIPTION: Pulse Thrusters are focused entirely on speed, at the expense of efficiency and maneuverability.

| TECH LEVEL | | | | |
|---|---|---|---|---|
| TOP SPEED | | | | |
| FLIGHT AGILITY | | | | |
| DODGE SPEED | | | | |
| RAM | | | | |

## AGILITY THRUSTERS

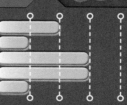

DESCRIPTION: Agility Thrusters greatly improve maneuverability with only moderate sacrifices to speed and efficiency.

| TECH LEVEL | | | | |
|---|---|---|---|---|
| TOP SPEED | | | | |
| FLIGHT AGILITY | | | | |
| DODGE SPEED | | | | |
| RAM | | | | |

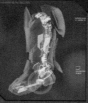

BASICS

ARMOR & UPGRADES

ENEMIES

MISSIONS

ONE MAN ARMY

SECRETS

## AEQUO THRUSTERS

DESCRIPTION: Aequo Thrusters are tuned for the most efficient and balanced transfer of power to speed. They offer good performance without excessive energy consumption.

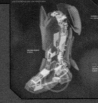

| | | | | |
|---|---|---|---|---|
| TECH LEVEL | | | | |
| TOP SPEED | | | | |
| FLIGHT AGILITY | | | | |
| DODGE SPEED | | | | |
| RAM | | | | |

## CELERITAS THRUSTERS

DESCRIPTION: Celeritas Thrusters are the fastest thruster system available. The incredible speed offered by this thruster system comes with reduction in agility.

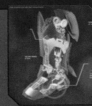

| | | | | |
|---|---|---|---|---|
| TECH LEVEL | | | | |
| TOP SPEED | | | | |
| FLIGHT AGILITY | | | | |
| DODGE SPEED | | | | |
| RAM | | | | |

## AGILITAS THRUSTERS

DESCRIPTION: The Agilitas Thruster system was built for maximum maneuverability at moderate speeds. These thrusters excel at rapidly changing direction and speed.

| | | | | |
|---|---|---|---|---|
| TECH LEVEL | | | | |
| TOP SPEED | | | | |
| FLIGHT AGILITY | | | | |
| DODGE SPEED | | | | |
| RAM | | | | |

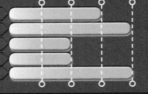

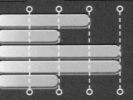

# ARMOR SUITS

New armor suits are unlocked by completing the main game, or by clearing One Man Army missions. Armor suits can be selected before starting a mission in Mission Archive and One Man Army modes.

Equipping various armor suits not only changes Iron Man's look, but also modifies his systems on a scale of one to five. Therefore, some great benefits can be had by equipping a different suit when replaying a mission or trying to clear One Man Army missions.

BASICS

ARMOR & UPGRADES

ENEMIES

MISSIONS

ONE MAN ARMY

SECRETS

## MARK III

**DESCRIPTION:** Designed for customization, the Mark III armor can be equipped with a variety of enhancements.

| | |
|---|---|
| ARMOR | |
| REPULSORS | |
| POWER SYSTEMS | |
| AUXILIARY WEAPONS | |
| MOBILITY | |

## CLASSIC

**DESCRIPTION:** Iron Man's first iconic armor debuted in *Tales of Suspense* #48 and underwent several subtle cosmetic changes before finalizing its look in *Tales of Suspense* #66. It was the first suit to feature the trademark palm-mounted repulsor rays.

| | |
|---|---|
| ARMOR | |
| REPULSORS | |
| POWER SYSTEMS | |
| AUXILIARY WEAPONS | |
| MOBILITY | |

*Unlock: Clear One Man Army vs. Mercs*

## EXTREMIS

**DESCRIPTION:** Used during major events such as *Civil War*, and appearing during the "Extremis" story arc, this armor represents Iron Man's modern look. In this suit, he has achieved new levels of power.

| | |
|---|---|
| ARMOR | |
| REPULSORS | |
| POWER SYSTEMS | |
| AUXILIARY WEAPONS | |
| MOBILITY | |

*Unlock: Clear One Man Army vs. Maggia*

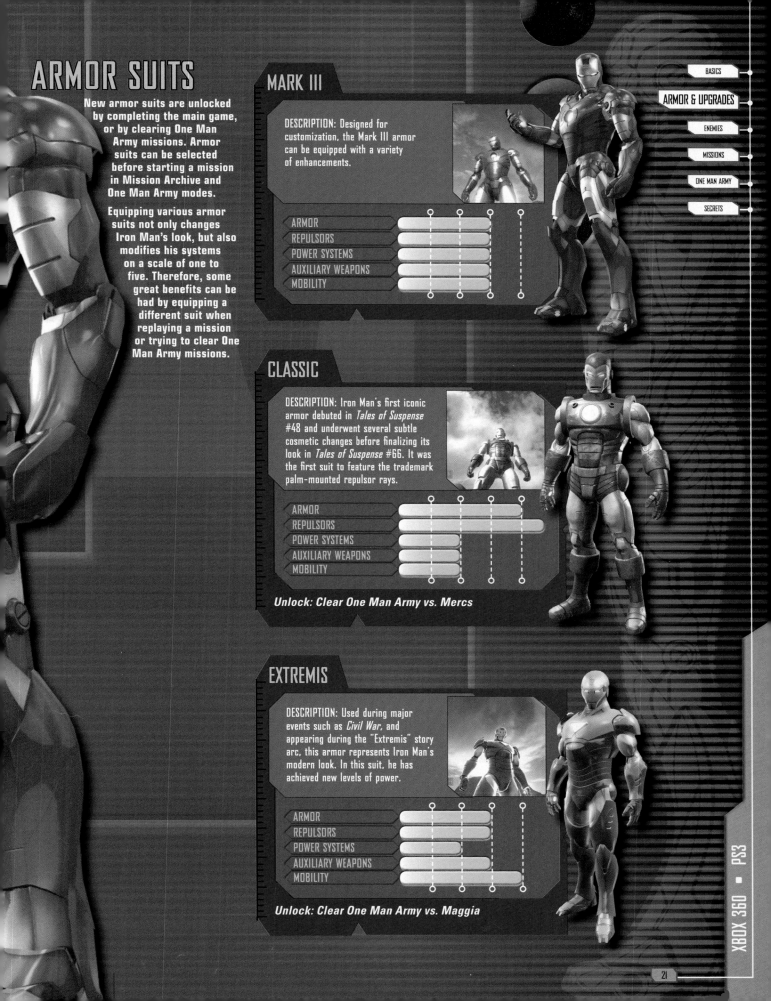

## MARK II ARMOR

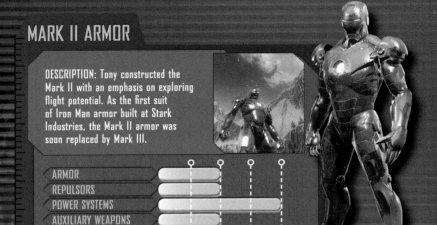

DESCRIPTION: Tony constructed the Mark II with an emphasis on exploring flight potential. As the first suit of Iron Man armor built at Stark Industries, the Mark II armor was soon replaced by Mark III.

| | | | | |
|---|---|---|---|---|
| ARMOR | | | | |
| REPULSORS | | | | |
| POWER SYSTEMS | | | | |
| AUXILIARY WEAPONS | | | | |
| MOBILITY | | | | |

**Unlock: Clear *One Man Army vs. Ten Rings***

## HULKBUSTER

DESCRIPTION: The name says it all. This, the first version of Iron Man's Hulkbuster armor, appeared in Iron Man #304, and greatly boosted the hero's strength and durability, enabling him to fight the Hulk one on one.

| | | | | |
|---|---|---|---|---|
| ARMOR | | | | |
| REPULSORS | | | | |
| POWER SYSTEMS | | | | |
| AUXILIARY WEAPONS | | | | |
| MOBILITY | | | | |

**Unlock: Clear *One Man Army vs. AIM-X*. Can also be unlocked when clear game save data from *Incredible Hulk* is stored on the same console.**

## SILVER CENTURION ▶ EXCLUSIVE TO THE XBOX 360™

DESCRIPTION: Sporting new colors, Tony used this suit during his fight with Iron Monger, his days as a West Coast Avenger, and in the first "Armor Wars" storyline.

| | | | | |
|---|---|---|---|---|
| ARMOR | | | | |
| REPULSORS | | | | |
| POWER SYSTEMS | | | | |
| AUXILIARY WEAPONS | | | | |
| MOBILITY | | | | |

**Unlock: Clear *Mission 13: Showdown***

ACTIVATE LIFE SUPPORT

BASICS

ARMOR & UPGRADES

ENEMIES

MISSIONS

ONE MAN ARMY

SECRETS

## CLASSIC MARK I

DESCRIPTION: The first-ever Iron Man suit was built during the character's initial appearance in *Tales of Suspense* #39, and this design originates from the interpretation from *Iron Man* Vol. 4 #5.

| | | | | |
|---|---|---|---|---|
| ARMOR | | | | |
| REPULSORS | | | | |
| POWER SYSTEMS | | | | |
| AUXILIARY WEAPONS | | | | |
| MOBILITY | | | | |

**Unlock: Clear *One Man Army vs. AIM***

## ULTIMATE ▶ EXCLUSIVE TO THE PLAYSTATION® 3

Description: In the Ultimate Universe, an alternate version of the Marvel Universe, Tony Stark requires the help of an entire specialized crew to help maintain this bulkier Iron Man armor. As seen in *The Ultimates*, this ensemble functions more like a compact vehicle than a man-sized suit of armor.

| | | | | |
|---|---|---|---|---|
| ARMOR | | | | |
| REPULSORS | | | | |
| POWER SYSTEMS | | | | |
| AUXILIARY WEAPONS | | | | |
| MOBILITY | | | | |

**Unlock: Clear *Mission 13: Showdown*.**

# ENEMIES

No matter which evil faction Iron Man squares off against, he always faces recognizable enemy types. To determine the type of enemy targeted at long range, refer to the Target Identification window in the upper right corner of the screen.

## ENEMY TYPES

### SOLDIER

Soldiers are human enemies that carry firearms, which do not inflict much damage to Iron Man as long as he has energy remaining. They are easily eradicated with a few shots of Iron Man's Main Weapon. Try to blow up squads of soldiers by detonating exploding barrels, by destroying nearby vehicles, or by dropping to the earth amidst a group to perform a Ground Pound.

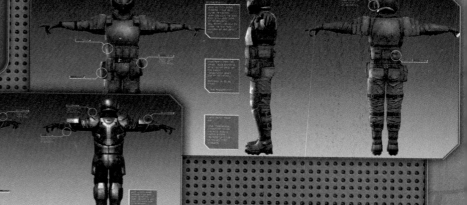

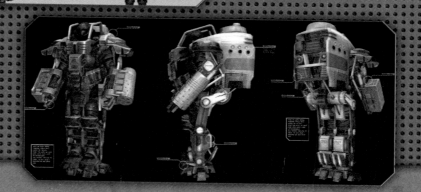

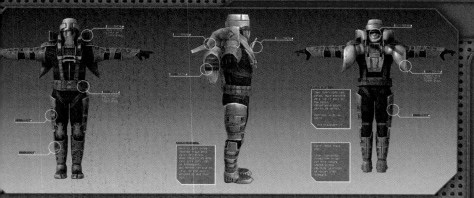

BASICS

ARMOR & UPGRADES

ENEMIES

MISSIONS

ONE MAN ARMY

SECRETS

# HOVER SOLDIER

Hover soldiers are equipped with jetpacks that enable them to fly. They typically carry powerful proton beam rifles, although some of them are equipped with missile launchers. Grappling a Hover soldier in midair replenishes life support more quickly.

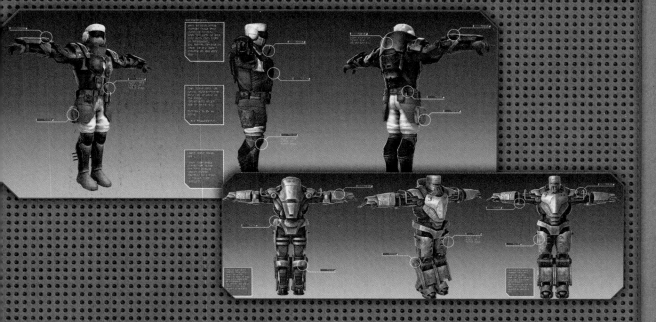

# BATTLE SUIT

These soldiers carry shoulder-fired missile launchers, some with homing capabilities. Battle Suits require several seconds to reload their launchers. They are stronger and require a few extra shots from Iron Man's weapons.

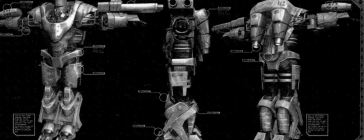

## FLAK TURRET

Flak turrets are rapid-firing cannons that fire a shrapnel spread which inflicts minor damage. They can be mounted to stationary trailers, towers, or to the rooftops of heavy terrain dune-buggies and jeeps. They are most effective against airborne targets. Flak turrets are lightly armored weapons, and typically can be easily destroyed with Repulsor fire. Flak can be extremely dangerous, but here's a tip! Look for the primary explosion and get out of the way before the secondary explosion detonates in the same location.

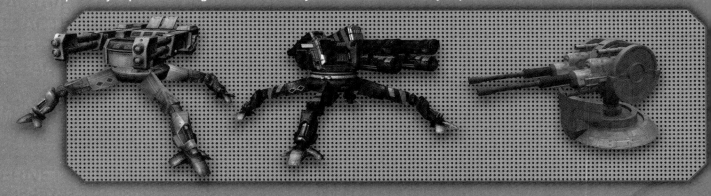

## MISSILE TURRET

Missile turrets fire rockets and homing missiles which explode on impact. They can be mounted on stationary trailers or towers. They are most effective against aerial targets. Missile turrets can be destroyed quickly with a combination of Auxiliary and Main Weapon fire. Missiles launched from turrets are numerous, but relatively easy to dodge by moving laterally. Learn to recognize the different missiles by their trails.

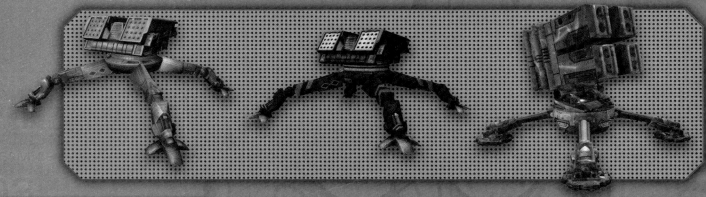

## APC

APCs (Armored Personnel Carriers) are fast-moving armored vehicles with a rotating turret fitted with a .50 caliber gun or grenade launcher. They are most effective against ground targets. They sometimes open to dispatch soldiers. APCs are more resilient than turrets, but not as strong as tanks. They can be easily destroyed with Melee attacks, or a combination of Auxiliary and Main Weapons.

BASICS

ARMOR & UPGRADES

ENEMIES

MISSIONS

ONE MAN ARMY

SECRETS

# TANK

Tanks are slow-moving armored vehicles with tracks and rotating turrets fitted with either 120mm cannons or prototype proton cannons. They are equally effective against ground or aerial targets. Tanks are incredibly resilient to damage, even melee attacks and grappling. Reroute power to melee or weapons appropriately when attacking a tank. Always use a combination of Repulsor and Auxiliary Weapon fire to take out tanks quickly and efficiently.

# SAM BATTERY

SAM (Surface-to-Air Missile) Batteries are mobile armored missile-launching platforms with anti-aircraft capabilities. They are only effective against flying or hovering targets. Although armored, SAMs can be destroyed more easily than tanks. Grapple a SAM Battery in order to take control of it, and then fire it at other targets to destroy them instantly!

# HOWITZER

Howitzers are short-barreled 105mm cannons that can be mounted to stationary trailers or small vehicles. They can target Iron Man on the ground or in the air. If you're forced onto the ground, don't stay in one place too long if Howitzers are around. They'll target you and nail you quickly. Destroy them easily with melee attacks, or a combination of Auxiliary and Main Weapons. Grapple howitzers to take control of them and fire them at other enemies.

# GUNSHIP

Gunship is a broad term used to classify any low-flying aerial attack craft encountered in the game, such as helicopters and AIM prototype rotor-wing craft. Gunships are capable of machinegun fire, missile launch, or proton cannon attack. They are effective against targets at any altitude below theirs, but are ineffective if Iron Man flies above them. They are easily destroyed with a combination of Auxiliary and Main Weapon, or by Grappling them from the ship's nose. Ramming a gunship at full speed using afterburners greatly damages or destroys them.

# DROPSHIP

Dropships are armored craft with no weapons used to drop off armored vehicles and/or soldiers. Dropships may deliver one squad or two. They typically fly toward Iron Man to make it difficult to target the vehicles and soldiers they drop off. Dropships are difficult to destroy, requiring several salvos of Auxiliary and Main Weapons and Unibeams to bring down. Dropships are too huge to be Grappled. Colliding with them midair while firing afterburners is a great way to damage them, but Iron Man also suffers in the process. Focus on taking out armed enemies before worrying about a dropship.

# FIGHTER

Fighters are jet aircraft that fly at high altitudes and attack with machinegun fire or proton cannon fire, and guided missiles. Their armor is light, and they are easy to destroy. However, their speed makes them difficult to pursue. The best strategy is to hover at high altitude and look for approaching missiles on your radar. Face the direction of the oncoming missile and dodge it, and then target the Fighter and fire Iron Man's Main Weapon. Turn to continue firing on the Fighter as it soars past. With power routed to your weapons, a Fighter cannot fly out of your range in time to avoid destruction. Fighters can also be Grappled in midair if you hover at a high altitude and time your Grapple to nab them. After Grappling a Fighter, press the Melee/Grapple button again with the right timing when the button icon appears onscreen to solidify your grasp on its wing. Once Iron Man grabs hold of the wing, he can aim the Fighter at the ground or other targets to inflict damage, and crash it.

# BOSSES

BASICS

ARMOR & UPGRADES

**ENEMIES**

MISSIONS

ONE MAN ARMY

SECRETS

Bosses are unique enemies that require specific strategies to defeat. Their attacks and weaknesses are detailed in the Mission walkthrough.

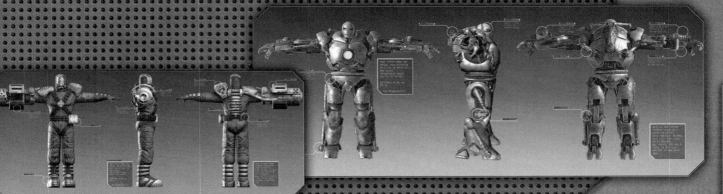

# ESCAPE

## MISSION DESCRIPTION

*A group of insurgents known as the Ten Rings has captured Tony Stark and commanded him to create the ultimate weapon for their evil goals. Instead, Stark forges an armored suit capable of withstanding a heavy barrage, armed with a Flamethrower and lock-on-enabled missiles. Tony dons the suit and emerges from the caves to confront his enemies and destroy the stolen Stark weapons caches.*

## PRIMARY OBJECTIVE

ESCAPE THE TEN RINGS ENCAMPMENT.

> ASSETS: 33

## HERO OBJECTIVE

DESTROY ALL OF THE STARK WEAPONS.

> ASSETS: 6

## BONUS OBJECTIVES

TIME CHALLENGE: 5:45

> ASSETS: 4

## ENEMIES TO DESTROY

ENEMIES TO DESTROY: 90

> ASSETS: 4

## NOTE YOUR VERSION!

This walkthrough covers the Xbox 360 and PlayStation 3 versions of *Iron Man*, played on Normal difficulty mode. Enemy appearances and event triggers are different in Easy and Hard modes.

## Scorch the Foot Soldiers

As Tony Stark dons the prototype Iron Man suit and attempts to blast his way out of the Ten Rings encampment, the first wave of resistance consists of machine-gun toting soldiers. Although machinegun fire inflicts little damage to Iron Man, continuous fire from several machineguns at once can significantly drain the suit. A suit failure occurs once it's been completely drained of residual armor and shows no life remaining. The suit can reboot three times before a mission failure happens. Failing the mission, you must restart from the very beginning. To avoid suit failure, move behind rocks, buildings, and other cover objects where enemy gunfire and missiles cannot reach. Taking cover allows the suit to restore Iron Man's health.

Press the Main Weapon button to use the Flamethrower, and douse the approaching soldiers with flames. While the arm cannon emits burning fuel, move the Look control to aim at targets. Each soldier dies immediately on contact with the fire spout, so there is no need to linger on a charred corpse. Be careful that you're not firing into the ground.

BASICS

ARMOR & UPGRADES

ENEMIES

MISSIONS

ONE MAN ARMY

SECRETS

## SUIT ENERGY METER NOT YET ONLINE

**The suit powers the Flamethrower. When the suit's power level drains, the Flamethrower sputters and cannot be used again until the suit recharges. The suit's energy meter is not visible onscreen until Tony's fellow captive and tech expert Yinsen engages the Life and Energy readout system via remote uplink. This event occurs shortly, so just play it by ear with the Flamethrower for the time being.**

## Instant Kills with Your Fists!

Iron Man's Melee attack is even more powerful and immediately effective than the Flamethrower is. When in close range, press the Melee/Grapple button to punch the nearest soldier. The attack sends the target flying and eliminates them instantly. Combine strategies by using the Flamethrower while approaching enemies, then use Melee attacks to finish off the last members of a squad in the most personal manner. You can also grapple soldiers by pressing and holding the Melee/Grapple button.

Continue making your way down the slope and eliminate all soldiers that appear.

## STAY ON YOUR TOES, LEAD FOOT!

**Continuous movement can help to reduce the amount of damage sustained by machinegun fire, and also improves mission time. Completing the mission within the Time Challenge displayed prior to accepting the mission awards additional Asset Points, which are used to upgrade Iron Man's suits.**

## Exploding Objects

A small dwelling at the bottom of the long slope divides the path. Soldiers behind sandbags placed around the building pour on the bullets. Steadily approach the central dwelling and use the Flamethrower to set the closest stack of oil barrels on fire. When the barrels explode, they cause surrounding barrel stacks to detonate as well. The resultant chain explosion wipes out the enemies near the central building as well as terrorists behind the sandbags on the left.

After the impressive fireworks display, head around the right side of the building and use the Flamethrower to detonate another stack of barrels to take out a duet, one of whom wields a missile launcher.

## Armor Buster!

Navigate down the slope and to the right. An APC (Armored Personnel Carrier) begins firing from around the corner. Rush it and strike its sides with Melee attacks before it can unload the soldiers it carries. Even if the soldiers do manage to disembark, the resulting explosion from smashing the APC kills the men on foot. Therefore, always go for the big, explosive machine rather than focus on singular enemies. Also keep in mind that Melee and Grapple attacks work much more efficiently against armored vehicles than weapons.

SYS005    01 3462 21
SYS006    00 1423 11

230
102
250
221

BIO ACTIVE
VENT ACTIVE

SYS005  01 3462 2109867 990
SYS006  00 1423 1122496 002

BIO  ACTIVE
VENT  ACTIVE
RESP  FLTR  ACTIVE
OPTIC  ACTIVE

||||||||    ||||||||||||||||

CYBERNET  9-4887-000-ARM
ROOT: 3845780672 DDL
../09: 290588394 303

PART GEN  7-4388 00
ROOT: 3842532372 OSU
../03: 290783394 -303

BOOT JET:23% ||||

771 DLP

UNI BEAM:49% |||| | | | ||

003 OMP

REP BEAM: ||||

675 %

SPEED
TNC.................... 32%
PLPT.................... 78%
PLPT....................

TEMP
ODS....................
FAN....................
SMO....................

LIFE SUPP
TYK....................

Continue around the corner to the left. When clashing against the second APC, try performing a Grapple. Move next to the APC's main body, then press and hold the Melee/Grapple button. Iron Man seizes the APC and begins to lift. The Melee/Grapple button icon flashes onscreen. Press the Melee/Grapple button rapidly to successfully complete the Grapple. Iron Man performs a custom takedown that destroys or significantly damages the armored vehicle. In the case of APC's, he flips them over and they explode!

### TAP WITH SUCCESS

To ensure that the Grapple is successful requires extremely rapid tapping of the Melee/Grapple button. In fact, you must tap the button as rapidly as possible, which is certainly more rapid than the average thumb can manage! To tap the button rapidly enough, we recommend using whichever finger/button combo works best to successfully destroy the target each time. This mini-game increases in difficulty along with the difficulty mode.

## Death's Alley

The narrow passage through the next area is choked with soldiers firing from both sides and an APC at the far end. Charging in with flames blazing is a sure way to trigger a suit failure. Instead, run diagonally across the area to the building ruins on the right side of the "alley". Move around the corner until gunfire is no longer hitting Iron Man, and wait there until his Life regenerates to full.

Head around the corner into the passage and use the Flamethrower to ignite the stacks of barrels. Destroying the barrels on the right side of the passage takes out the soldier on the ground and the rocket launcher above, and destroying the barrels on the far side causes an explosion chain reaction that takes out all the soldiers on the left side as well as the tank at the far end!

## Energy Systems Online!

As Iron Man proceeds toward the distant bridge, Yinsen finally gets the suit's energy core online. With the energy core supplying power to the suit, Iron Man can finally monitor the energy drain of the Flamethrower. Keep an eye on this readout as you continue down the passageway, taking out the terrorists on foot who attempt to block your path.

Shortly thereafter, Yinsen also activates the suit's targeting and lock-on systems. Targeting markers appear on each enemy and armored unit. To lock-on to a target, move the Look control so that the central crosshair touches a target marker and changes it to a large circle. The curved bar on the left side of the lock-on marker indicates the target's remaining health or structural integrity.

BASICS

ARMOR & UPGRADES

ENEMIES

MISSIONS

ONE MAN ARMY

SECRETS

Continue forward and use the Flamethrower and Melee attacks on the four terrorists standing in a line. When they die, Yinsen manages to activate the missile launch system, and just in time. Use the Look control to tilt your view upward to the vehicles on the bridge. A transport truck is overturned next to a tank. Target the overturned truck on the left and press the Auxiliary Weapon button to fire a missile at it. When the truck explodes, it also destroys the tank too, whereas two or more missiles must be fired at the tank to destroy it alone. As flaming debris rains from the bridge, continue following the passage beneath the bridge to the next area.

## The Stockpile

Kill a few more foot soldiers and continue following the passage. After rounding a corner to the left, the first of the Stark weapon stockpiles comes into view. The stockpiles are highlighted with orange target markers and lock-on markers to indicate that they are objective targets. Lock onto and fire a Missile at the central stockpile. The explosion triggers a chain reaction that takes out several pallets at once.

Continue around the corner and use Missiles to destroy the tank firing from the far end. The circular indicator next to the energy meter in the lower left corner of the screen indicates when the next Missile will be ready to launch. When the circle is full, press the Auxiliary Weapon button to fire another Missile at the tank. Take cover while the Missile reloads to avoid taking too much damage in the meantime.

Avoid moving too far out to the left to prevent taking damage from some soldiers guarding another stockpile tucked between some buildings in a niche to the right. After the tank is destroyed, target and destroy the stockpile, and the soldiers easily go up with it.

## Wide Open Dunes

Head into the next region, sticking to the right as you proceed. Kill the soldier with a rocket launcher around the corner, and then move to the top of the dune and stop. Terrorists race down the slope on the far right. As they descend, target the weapon stockpile at the base of the slope and shoot a Missile at it to take out all the soldiers at once. Then make your way toward the slope.

A helicopter zooms into the fray as you navigate up the slope. Ignore it for the moment and target the barrels at the top of the slope. Shooting the stack on the right takes out the soldier with the rocket launcher. Proceed to a spot near the top of the slope.

Gaining some altitude helps in targeting and fighting the helicopter, which can be brought down easily with single locked-on Missile.

230
102
250
221

21
11

BIO ACTIVE
VENT ACTIVE

SYS005     01 3462 2109867 990
SYS006     00 1423 1122496 002

BIO ACTIVE
VENT ACTIVE
RESP FLTR
OPTIC ACT

|||||||||   |||||||||

CYBERNET
ROOT: 3845782   303
.../09: 290582   303

PART GEN 7 4333 002 FRT
ROOT: 384253   303
.../03: 290783394 303

BOOT JET:23%

771 DL

UNI BEAM:49%

003 OMP

REP BEAM: |||| |

675 %

SPEED
TNC.................
PLPT................
PLPT................

TEMP
ODS................
FAN................
SMO................

LIFE SUPP
TYK................12%

Now look to the far side of the plain to see a tank moving back and forth on the distant hill. Shoot either the tank or the barrels, and then shoot the tank again to blow it up.

Descend the slope and follow along the next canyon. Use Missiles to take out rocket launcher-armed soldiers along the way, as well as an APC. Don't miss a small pocket of enemies to the far right, firing missiles from atop an insurmountable rise.

## Finally, Some Shade!

Use Missiles to take out the soldiers blocking the tunnel entrance to the next area. Use your Flamethrower on additional terrorists inside so that your missile may reload. Then use a Grapple attack to destroy the tank blocking the tunnel exit.

Run from cover point to cover point as you fire missiles at the two tanks at the far end of the next passageway, waiting for your missiles to reload each time. When one tank is destroyed, it is then safe to approach and Grapple the other tank. Allow your Missile to reload and your Life to regenerate before dropping off the steep bluff into the next area.

BASICS

ARMOR & UPGRADES

ENEMIES

MISSIONS

ONE MAN ARMY

SECRETS

# RAZA

**1** Tony Stark's former captor is piloting the newest in Stark Industries' line of deadly, heavily reinforced tanks. The only strategy necessary is to avoid the tank's cannon blasts while firing Missiles at it. The tank follows a pre-determined path through the area, and almost immediately moves along a line of fuel tanks. Target and shoot the fuel tanks to inflict greater damage to Raza's tank than missiles alone can do. When the energy gauge of Raza's tank is down to 20% or less, approach and Grapple it for the win!

**2** Note that helicopters reappear continuously in the southwest corner of Raza's area. Check the Mission Pause menu, and if your kill count is too low to achieve the bonus, fluff it by destroying several helicopters before finishing Raza off. Scan the southern skyline as soon as you see the helicopter's icon appear on your radar.

## ACHIEVE BONUS OBJECTIVES IN THE MISSION ARCHIVE!

Accumulating the enemy kill quota and completing the mission in the time allotted is nearly impossible, especially your first time out. Luckily, each completed mission becomes playable in the Mission Archive menu on the title screen. By replaying the mission, you can achieve Bonus Objectives and win additional assets.

Completing the first mission in 6:40 is possible if you run through and defeat Raza as quickly as possible. But it is almost impossible to eliminate 98 enemies in such a short amount of time.

To raise your kill count, avoid attacking Raza and simply keep destroying the endless helicopters appearing in the boss's area. Destroying roughly ten choppers should do the trick. Raza does not count as a regular enemy, so destroy helicopters until your kill count reaches 98. The total enemies destroyed is listed on the Mission Pause menu. Press the Pause button to view this screen.

SYS001      00 0098 230

SYS002      00 7802 102

SYS003      01 6730 250

SYS004      00 7349 22

SYS005      01 3462 21

SYS006      00 1423 11

BIO  ACTIVE

VENT  ACTIVE

# 2 FIRST FLIGHT

## MISSION DESCRIPTION

*Returning to Stark Industries following his harrowing ordeal, Tony Stark resolves to hone and improve the design of the Iron Man armor. The Mark II armor boasts a sleek design and flight capabilities, all controlled with the assistance of a combat AI named Jarvis. Time for a flight test!*

## PRIMARY OBJECTIVE

DEFEND STARK INDUSTRIES FROM MAGGIA ATTACK.

ASSETS: 40

## HERO OBJECTIVE

DESTROY DRONES WITHOUT CIVILIAN DAMAGE.

ASSETS: 2 (X4)

## BONUS OBJECTIVES

TIME CHALLENGE: 7:30

ASSETS: 4

## ENEMIES TO DESTROY

ENEMIES TO DESTROY: 70

ASSETS: 4

## *Hover and Rise*

Flight is easy to control in the Mark II armor suit! The first objective is to hover in place for three seconds. To hover, depress the Hover button halfway. Tony rises off the rooftop slightly and hovers in the air. While hovering, you can slowly move any direction using the Move control. Hover for three seconds in order to proceed with the mission.

On Jarvis's cue, fully depress the Hover button to continuously gain altitude. Continue rising for three seconds, until Jarvis speaks again.

## *Thrusters*

When Jarvis prompts, press and hold the Fly button to engage Iron Man's thrusters. While flying, use the Move control to govern your flight pitch and yaw, and to acceleration into a turn.

BASICS

ARMOR & UPGRADES

ENEMIES

MISSIONS

ONE MAN ARMY

SECRETS

After Tony orders Jarvis to bring the thrusters online, press the Dodge/Boost button to engage Iron Man's thrusters. The thrusters accelerate flight speed, but deplete the suit's energy meter. When the energy meter runs dry, Iron Man returns to normal flight speed until the suit regenerates energy. Iron Man cannot engage thrusters again until the energy meter is filled past the thruster indicator on the energy meter (the icon that resembles the bottom of Iron Man's rocket boots).

## Marker to Marker

After flying successfully in any direction for five seconds, glide toward the glowing blue holographic marker, which Jarvis projects over a small building beside a tall skyscraper in south portion of the stage. The marker's position is indicated by an orange dot in the distance, an orange target marker at closer range, and an orange indicator on Iron Man's radar in the lower right corner of the screen. If Iron Man is not facing the marker, an orange arrow appears at the peripheral of the screen indicating the best direction to turn in order to locate the marker.

Keep flying toward the marker until Iron Man gets close enough that it disappears. Another marker appears above the taller building to Iron Man's left. The next marker appears above the chemical processing plant to the southeast. Then fly toward the subsequent markers at the following positions:

- ○ **In the narrow gap between the tallest chemical tanks at the plant,**
- ○ **To the west, over the water's surface,**
- ○ **To the northwest, beside a dock crane,**
- ○ **A little farther northwest, hovering beneath a bridge. Do not engage afterburners while flying under the bridge. You might accidentally collide with the bridge or the water's surface,**
- ○ **To the northeast, behind some very tall buildings,**
- ○ **Due east, hovering over the street near some tall buildings,**
- ○ **And finally, hovering over the skyscraper behind the architectural building with the green roof and the chapel tower.**

## PILOTING REQUIRES SUBTLETY IN CONTROL!

Only very slight adjustments of the Move control are needed to manage flight, and moving the control too far makes flight navigation more difficult.

## MODERATION WITH AFTERBURNERS

Using afterburners makes flight harder to control, since the slightest change or error in pitch or yaw can cause Iron Man to collide with a surface before you even see the danger. Such collisions inflict self-damage. Avoid engaging the afterburners when flying near the ground or the surface of water, or when flying near buildings, cliffs, tall bridges, and other objects.

BIO ACTIVE
VENT ACTIVE

## Aerial Combat Training

When the flying portion of training is complete, fly toward the new marker floating high above the windmill area. Hover in that position and wait for three combat drones to approach. When the drones reach their positions, one of them fires a missile at Iron Man.

To dodge the missile, move left or right while hovering and press the Dodge/Boost button to dodge the attack with a short rocket burst.

Next, try to Grapple a missile just before it strikes Iron Man by pressing the Grapple/Melee button. Time your button press to the instant just after the lock-on marker appears around the missile. Turn around until you have the target in your crosshairs and then release the missile to complete the training.

## Aerial Grapple

The next exercise is a bit trickier. The drones reposition themselves, and you must Grapple the one marked with a target indicator. Use the Move control while hovering to close in on the drone, and fully depress the Hover button to achieve short elevations in height, until Iron Man is hovering next to the drone. Then press the Grapple/Melee button to engage the drone in a mid-air Grapple. Rapidly tap the button as the onscreen icon indicates to tear the drone's wings off.

## Power Routing Allocation

Jarvis brings the Power Routing system online. By pressing the directional buttons on the controller as indicated onscreen, you can reroute the power of Iron Man's energy to support the systems of Iron Man's armor. The energy subsystems are (in clockwise order from the top or up direction):

- **Life Support**: Iron Man regains lost health more quickly. He is also less likely to suffer damage from minor attacks.

- **Melee**: Iron Man inflicts greater damage with Melee and Grapple attacks.

- **Weapons**: Iron Man's weapons inflict greater damage and fire more rapidly than usual.

- **Thrusters**: Iron Man can fly with afterburners engaged and not consume energy.

To continue the mission, reroute Iron Man's power to any subsystem. We recommend rerouting to Thrusters for now, to prepare for the next event.

## Unibeam Analysis

While locked-on to the last remaining drone, press and hold the Unibeam button to charge up the Unibeam attack. When ready, release the button to unleash the Unibeam and destroy the drone. Charging up the Unibeam consumes some of Iron Man's energy meter. Charging the Unibeam too much drains some of Iron Man's life support. Later upgrades to the Iron Man armor can increase the damaging power and firing speed of the Unibeam, at a greater cost in energy.

BASICS

ARMOR & UPGRADES

ENEMIES

MISSIONS

ONE MAN ARMY

SECRETS

## Maggia Attacks!

Training is over, just in time for some practical application of the techniques you've learned. While hovering, turn back to face the Stark Industries building at the center of the city. When explosions erupt, engage your thrusters and afterburners.

Reroute power to your thrusters to avoid consuming all your energy during the trip. Fly toward the orange target marker.

When Iron Man comes upon the enemy forces, disengage thrusters and hover in the air above. Reroute power to your weapons. Fire your Main Weapon and Missiles in combo to take out several Maggia Tanks in the area, all marked with orange. Use your radar to anticipate and dodge missiles fired from your sides or behind.

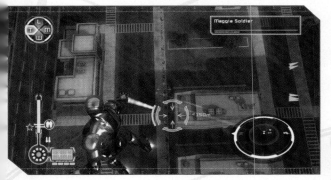

Around this time, Maggia Gunships fly in from the south to drop ground forces. Use afterburners to streak south to a grass hill where three Maggia SAM Batteries are parked, unleashing barrages of missiles. Grapple one of the SAM batteries to take control of it. Use the

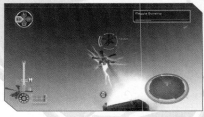

Look control to aim the SAM at one of the helicopters, and press your Main Weapon button to fire the SAM. Destroy the remaining gunships by firing your weapons at them, or by moving in close range and Grappling them from the front.

### THE DIRECT APPROACH

Another clever disposal method for helicopters is to fly directly at them with your afterburners engaged. The collision force destroys the gunship!

## Incoming Ground Troops

Following the gunship drop assault, orange target markers appear at the outskirts of the area and Jarvis warns of incoming ground forces. Reroute power to your thrusters and take off after any of the orange markers. Disengage afterburners as you approach and start pelting the APCs at these locations with missiles and your main weapon. Gunships may move in to inhibit your assault, but try to focus on enemies marked in orange as opposed to blue. Continue flying to the far edges of the map and destroy the APCs to proceed in the mission.

### MAXIMUM IMPACT

Inflict massive damage simply by dropping out of the air next to these transports, releasing a shock wave that damages all targets in the vicinity!

SYS005   01 3462 21
SYS006   00 1423 11

BIO  ACTIVE
VENT ACTIVE

SYS005      01 3462 2109867 990
SYS006      00 1423 1122496 002
BIO  ACTIVE
VENT  ACTIVE
RESP  FLTR  ACTIVE
OPTIC  ACTIVE

CYBERNET  2-4987-0
ROOT: 3845782372 OSU
.../09: 290582

PART GEN
ROOT: 384253
.../03: 290789

BOOT JET:23%

## Dropships Inbound

With the ground troops eliminated, several sets of dual Maggia Dropships appear at the north, south, west, and east ends of the area. Reroute power to thrusters and use afterburners to reach them ASAP. These are quite a bit more durable than average helicopters. Reroute power to your weapons when in range and fire missiles and Unibeam attacks to take them out as quickly as possible. Kill any Maggia Missile Soldiers they leave behind, in order to continue advancing in the mission.

# STARK GUNSHIP

**1** The Maggia Dropship assault subsides just as one of the enemy soldiers somehow sneaks into a secure Stark Industry hangar and steals Tony's most advance fighter jet prototype. The Gunship pilot is an extremely low flier, so avoid hovering too high out of range. However, do not follow the gunship into the maze of buildings, or you may collide with a few of them by accident. Reroute power to your weapons as long as he is within lock-on distance. Do not attempt to Grapple with the Gunship, since it simply does not work. Pelt it from above with Missiles and your Repulsors. Use your regular thrusters to pursue the pilot as needed.

**2** When the Gunship's pilot decides it's time, he releases three drones set to attack the civilian population. The longer the drones are left alone, the more civilian damage they cause. Jarvis announces when the drones have inflicted casualties. Break off pursuing the Stark Gunship. Destroy the drones to protect the populace and achieve additional asset points. Each drone can easily be destroyed with a shot or two of your main weapon. Then return to dodging the Stark Gunship's missiles and countering with salvos of your own until the battle is finished.

BASICS

ARMOR & UPGRADES

ENEMIES

MISSIONS

ONE MAN ARMY

SECRETS

## MISSION WRAP-UP

| NEW TECH AVAILABLE |
|---|
| **CORE SYSTEMS UPGRADE (TECH LEVEL 2)** |
| IMPROVED MARK III SYSTEM |
| STRIKER SYSTEM |
| **MOBILITY ENHANCEMENTS UPGRADE (TECH LEVEL 2)** |
| ADVANCED CORE THRUSTERS |
| PULSE THRUSTERS |
| AGILITY THRUSTERS |

### SUIT CONFIGURATION: PRE-MISSION 03

Now that Tony Stark has designed the modifiable Mark III suit, you now have the option to implement upgrades to the design prior to each subsequent mission from here forward. Highlight a system to view the current Tech Level, funds available for upgrades, and each system module currently equipped (on the right side of the screen).

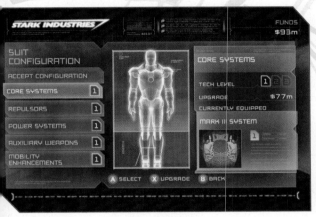

Press the Select button as shown onscreen to view detailed information on each system, including (from left to right, top to bottom):

- Modules Available and their Tech Levels
- Diagram of Placement on the Armor
- Description of the Module
- System Statistics that vary based on System Viewed

To upgrade a system, highlight it in the first screen and press the Upgrade button as displayed. After confirming that you will spend tens of million of dollars to purchase the upgrade; new modules become available for the selected system.

Because of system interdependency, only the Core Systems and Mobility Enhancements can initially be upgraded. Upgrading Core Systems makes more durable armor modules available, decreasing the amount of damage sustained from hits and also improving melee attack power. Upgrading Mobility Enhancements unlocks new modules that increase flight and dodge speed, as well as ramming damage.

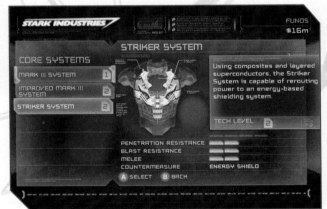

We strongly recommend upgrading the Core Systems to Tech Level 2 in order to improve your armor's durability. With this upgrade, you may equip either the Improved Mark III System module or the Striker System module. Improved Mark III greatly improves protection against firearm bullets and melee attacking strength, and also adds the chaff missile defense countermeasure (press the Countermeasure button to activate). The Striker System slightly improves both bullet and missile resistance, raises melee strength, and also activates the energy shield countermeasure that erects a mild force field around Iron Man when the Countermeasure button is pressed. The energy shield reduces the energy meter when in effect.

Highlight "Accept Configuration" at the top of the Suit Configuration screen and press the Select button to proceed.

# STARK WEAPONS

## MISSION DESCRIPTION

*Finishing his business with the Ten Rings, Iron Man returns to the arid region where he was formerly imprisoned. Now donning the vastly improved Mark III armor, his mission is to wipe out the stockpiles of stolen Stark Industries weapons. And if the Ten Rings' hardware happens to get in the way, then he is ready to deal with them, too!*

## PRIMARY OBJECTIVE

DESTROY STARK WEAPONS STOCKPILES.

ASSETS: 61

## HERO OBJECTIVE

DEFEAT US FIGHTERS WITHOUT HARMING THE PILOTS.

ASSETS: 14

## BONUS OBJECTIVES

TIME CHALLENGE: 9:00

ASSETS: 6

## ENEMIES TO DESTROY

ENEMIES TO DESTROY: 100

ASSETS: 6

## *Avatar of Destruction*

From the starting point, fly down into the valley directly ahead and toward the orange target indicators. Immediately you will notice that the defenses positioned there are extremely effective against an aerial approach. The best strategy is therefore to take on this installation from the ground. Press the Dodge/Boost button quickly twice while flying to execute an evasive barrel-roll as you descend. Land on the ground beside the closest SAM Battery to destroy it with the impact shock.

Grapple the other SAM Battery and point it at other defensive mechanisms to take them out. As the area clears up, launch missiles into the open warehouse and all over the roof to take out the weapon stockpiles.

Fly up out of the canyon and to the right, and take on the next installation on the ridge high above. The forces located here are not as strong against an aerial target, so hover over the location and rain down destruction from above. Destroy the stockpiles behind the exterior wall in the yard as well as the pallets in the open warehouse.

Continue flying along the canyon and destroy the stockpiles at each installation you come upon. Execute ground attacks

against stockpiles guarded by missile-launching SAM Batteries, and take out stockpiles guarded by tanks from above.

## We Got a Trucking Convoy!

When the last stockpiles are destroyed, the terrorists load the most advanced Stark explosives onto convoy trucks and try to flee the area. Fly to each convoy's location marked with an orange dot on the radar and destroy the convoy truck and any escort vehicles.

BASICS

ARMOR & UPGRADES

ENEMIES

MISSIONS

ONE MAN ARMY

SECRETS

## STANDARD COMBAT APPROACH

When approaching any cluster of enemy ground forces from the air, stop and hover at far enough range that only one or two enemies have blue target markers at a time. As you destroy outlying enemies, gradually hover or descend farther into the cluster and continue pouring on the juice. Maintain continuous fire with your Repulsors, and launch Missiles whenever ready to break up ground forces more quickly. With just a few units remaining, start firing Unibeams to wrap things up.

## WORKING ON BONUS OBJECTIVES

Especially when attempting to achieve the Time Challenge bonus or trying to unlock Xbox 360 Achievements, ignore the blue-marked units surrounding objectives such as the convoy vehicles. When attempting to kill the required number of enemies for the other bonus, destroy armored vehicles quickly by firing Missiles and follow up with a fully-charged Unibeam. Pepper lesser targets like turret guns with fire from your right-hand Repulsor.

BIO ACTIVE
VENT ACTIVE

# DREADNOUGHT

**1** With all their defensive measures in ruins, the terrorists launch their most terrifying armored vehicle: the Dreadnought. So many guns and cannons are attached to the hood of this thing that attacking from the front or above is a suicide mission. Instead, fly to the rear of the craft and attack from behind. Target the Dreadnought's rotor engines on the upper rear portion of the vehicle. Destroying the rotors converts the Dreadnought into a massive paperweight.

**2** Next, gradually move forward along the sides of the immobilized vehicle and destroy the auto guns and turrets to lighten the anti-air defenses. With these gone, the Dreadnought can still launch missiles. However, missiles alone can be dodged or grappled and "returned to sender" to inflict damage on the Dreadnought's central systems.

**3** Finish off the Dreadnought from above by targeting the hatch marked with orange in the center of the vehicle. Bombard the hatch with missiles and Unibeams. Allow yourself to drop back to the ground between each attack to reduce the amount of damage sustained from missiles. When the hatch is eradicated, repeat the same strategy to destroy the Dreadnought's core. Destroying the core junks the Dreadnought.

003 OMP

REP BEAM: IIII II III II

675 %

SPEED
TNC..................... 32%
PLPT.................... 78%
PLPT.................... 78%

TEMP
ODS....................
FAN....................
SMO....................

LIFE SUPPORT
TYK.................... 13%

## Military Intervention

Ignorant of Tony's intentions, three Air Force fighter jets arrive on the scene to intercept Iron Man. They appear on the radar as yellow circles to indicate that they are optional targets. If you wish to complete the mission quickly to achieve the Time Bonus objective, simply shoot down the fighters.

However, doing so causes you to lose a significant amount of assets for the mission and forfeit the Hero Objective.

The best, albeit trickiest, way to handle the situation is to try to grapple the jets and force the pilots to eject. Unfortunately an aerial chase is out of the question, since Iron Man cannot match or exceed the jet's speed even with Tech Level 2 Mobility Enhancement modules. The best strategy is to hover at the highest altitude possible and watch the jets carefully as they swoop in toward Iron Man's position.

The jets typically fly directly at Iron Man, and usually fire a missile in advance. Absorb the missile damage, since dodging puts you out of the jet's path. When the jet is in range, press the Melee/Grapple button to seize the aircraft's wing.

The only thing left to do is aim the fighter at a cliff or bridge using the Look control, and ground it permanently. The pilot safely ejects just before the crash.

Repeat this tactic with the other two fighter jets to complete the mission and gain a large bonus in assets.

BASICS

ARMOR & UPGRADES

ENEMIES

MISSIONS

ONE MAN ARMY

SECRETS

# ONE MAN ARMY MODE UNLOCKED!

One Man Army mode becomes unlocked upon completion of *Mission 03*. The first level available is One Man Army vs. Ten Rings. This new mode is available from the start menu. The objective of One Man Army is to defeat all enemies before the time limit expires. New armor suits and upgrades become available by completing One Man Army missions, so take a break from story mode once in a while!

## MISSION WRAP-UP

| NEW TECH AVAILABLE |
| --- |
| POWER SYSTEMS UPGRADE (TECH LEVEL 2) |
| MICRO FUSION |
| CONVERTER AUGMENTED |

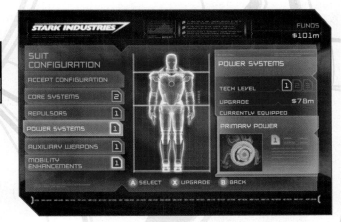

## SUIT CONFIGURATION: PRE-MISSION 04

Modules newly available allow upgrading of the Power System to Tech Level 2 for $78 million. However, prior to Mission 04 we strongly recommend spending your hard earned assets to upgrade the Mobility Enhancements system to Tech Level 2 for $70 million. Equip either the Advanced Core Thrusters or the Pulse Thrusters to improve your top speed. The stage in Mission 04 is a wide open area with several mountains as flight obstacles. Faster thrusters help to get the job done more quickly with fewer civilian casualties!

## MISSION DESCRIPTION

*Stark has learned that his disgruntled former clients, the Maggia, are developing weapons derived from Stark Industries technology and selling them to criminal organizations. Donning his iconic armor once again, Iron Man sets off to destroy the Maggia's production facilities. Unfortunately, these factories are nestled amid civilian areas. Iron Man must prevent the Maggia from covering their tracks by eliminating their own workforce.*

## PRIMARY OBJECTIVE

DESTROY THE MAGGIA FACTORIES.

ASSETS: 73

## HERO OBJECTIVE

PROTECT THE WAREHOUSE WORKERS.

ASSETS: 2 (X4)

## BONUS OBJECTIVES

TIME CHALLENGE: 7:00

ASSETS: 7

## ENEMIES TO DESTROY

ENEMIES TO DESTROY: 75

ASSETS: 7

## Take Out the Leadership

Fly northeast (according to the mini-radar displayed onscreen) from the starting point to reach the closest Maggia headquarters location. The HQ is highlighted with an orange target marker. The surrounding AA (Anti-Aircraft) Turrets and Missile Turrets are optional targets, but taking them out ensures that they cannot attack you from behind as you move over to clear out the central warehouse area. A Maggia Tank on the connecting bridge nearby is also a good target for elimination.

### IN AND OUT

To speed up playing time and try to score the Time Challenge bonus, hover well outside the small areas surrounding each target location and fire a couple of Unibeams to destroy the headquarters buildings. Ignore all other targets and move on.

## Artillery Central

Although the other factories await, instead, fly over to the central civilian warehouses area to pick apart the heavy concentration of ordinance there. Doing so prevents gunships and missiles fired from the civilian warehouses area from pursuing you while completing your objectives. Although Jarvis recommends against it, clearing out the area also stands to make the rest of the mission much easier. Just keep an eye on your life support meter as you pick off the armaments, and fly away to recoup if necessary.

MISSION 05

BASICS

ARMOR & UPGRADES

ENEMIES

MISSIONS

ONE MAN ARMY

SECRETS

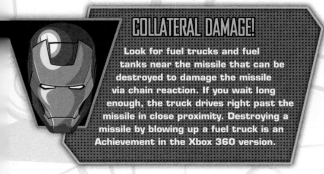

## COLLATERAL DAMAGE!

Look for fuel trucks and fuel tanks near the missile that can be destroyed to damage the missile via chain reaction. If you wait long enough, the truck drives right past the missile in close proximity. Destroying a missile by blowing up a fuel truck is an Achievement in the Xbox 360 version.

## Central Power

After Iron Man deals with the three rocket launch attempts, Jarvis detects that a large, indestructible pulse cannon above the mansion has been activated. The only way to disable it is by destroying the power core beneath the mansion.

Fly toward the central area, maintaining an extremely low altitude so that the pulse cannon cannot hit you. Fly through the extremely deep chasm that runs beneath and just behind the mansion. The power core is tucked under the bridge, and is heavily defended by AA and Missile Turrets as well as new tanks and SAM Batteries rolling into the area. Approach the situation gingerly, eliminating outlying turrets and tanks before moving inward. Eradicate most of the threats in the area surrounding the orange-marked power core before targeting it. Destroying the core blows up the mansion, and achieves victory in yet another mission on Iron Man's long road to peace!

## MISSION WRAP-UP

### NEW TECH AVAILABLE
**AUXILIARY WEAPONS UPGRADE (TECH LEVEL 2))**
**AEGAEON MICRO-GRENADES**
**VESPID MISSILES**

## SUIT CONFIGURATION: PRE-MISSION 06

If you have missed out on assets by not completing Hero Objectives or Bonus Objectives in previous missions, now is the time to atone. Select previous missions from the Mission Archive screen, and replay them in order to achieve criteria previously failed or overlooked. Iron Man needs to be as beefy as he can get for the next mission.

Power is a key factor in Mission 06, more so than the newly-available Auxiliary Weapons system upgrade. If you have avoided upgrades at all, please upgrade your Core, Mobility, Power, and Repulsors systems all to Tech Level 2 before continuing.

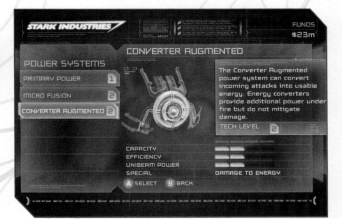

## MISSION DESCRIPTION

*As the Maggia Compound explodes in flames, Jarvis detects the launch of a massive aerial vehicle. The Maggia attempt to escape in their unbelievably huge flying fortress, with the intention of flying over the sea and attacking the population. Iron Man must take out the flying fortress and sink it before the Maggia can exact their terrifying revenge and innocent people suffer.*

## PRIMARY OBJECTIVE

DESTROY THE FLYING FORTRESS.

ASSETS: 88

## HERO OBJECTIVE

AVOID CIVILIAN CASUALTIES.

ASSETS: 19

## BONUS OBJECTIVES

TIME CHALLENGE: 7:00

ASSETS: 9

## ENEMIES TO DESTROY

ENEMIES TO DESTROY: 58

ASSETS: 9

## On Approach

As displayed onscreen, Iron Man has twenty minutes to bring down the Maggia's flying fortress before it reaches the population and begins inflicting civilian casualties. Immediately reroute power to the thrusters and engage your afterburners.

As you streak toward the Maggia's ultimate weapon, the ship's cannons begin firing anti-aircraft concussion grenades that explode mid-air, creating a net of damaging shrapnel. To avoid damage, turn hard to the left or right as you fly toward the fortress. Once again, just like fire from flak turrets, watch for the initial explosion and avoid the area because a second explosion is going to hit that same location right after. The closer you get to the target, the more intense the salvos become. Press the Dodge/Boost button while flying to the left or right to barrel-roll and hopefully avoid some damage.

A trio of Maggia Gunships hover a short distance between Iron Man and the fortress. Ignore them and continue gunning your afterburners to reach the main ship. Fly toward the top of the central structure, and glide over the roof.

BASICS

ARMOR & UPGRADES

ENEMIES

MISSIONS

ONE MAN ARMY

SECRETS

## Central Turrets

Jarvis highlights all of the fortress's main defense weapons. Naturally, they are all firing proton beam technology developed by Stark. You must destroy ten of them in order to proceed. Eliminating secondary targets is also beneficial, to reduce the amount of damage Iron Man sustains per second.

The Maggia Turrets highlighted in orange are extremely durable. The best approach is to land on the surface of the fortress next to the turrets and smash or grapple them. Reroute power to your melee systems to ensure that grapples work against the proton beam turrets. The gunships you ignored while flying to the fortress swarm about, so enjoy the party!

As your view of the wing deepens, you'll notice a heptagonal "helipad" on the surface. This is one of two bays that the Maggia Gunships emanate from. Fire a Unibeam to destroy the bay, and then use Repulsors and Missiles to take out the Missile Turrets so that your flights across the wings are less dangerous. Stick close enough to the outside wall of the sloping trench so that only one Missile Turret is visible at a time, reducing the number of enemies firing upon you as you work to clear the rear wing. When finished on one side, run back along the trench to the other side and destroy all the missile turrets and the helipad there.

### INCREASING ENEMY KILL COUNT

During this mission, if you wish to destroy enough enemies to fulfill the bonus objective then leave the helipads well enough alone. Without the continually appearing gunships, there are not enough easily destructible targets to accumulate the required count.

## Destroy the Helipads

After destroying the turrets on the central rooftop, continue running toward the back of the fortress. Just before reaching the massive hatch the covers the central reactor, you should reach a narrow "trench" that runs across the curved spine of the ship. Drop into this niche, and run toward either side of the ship.

## Clear the Wings

After taking out the missile turrets on the rear platforms of the body, fly along the top of either wing set and eliminate the turrets marked in orange.

SYS005    01 3462 21
SYS006    00 1423 11

BIO  ACTIVE
VENT  ACTIVE

When the top surface is clear, fly over the front of the wing to the dark area between the upper and lower wings. There are two turrets mounted on the top of the lower wing, close to the center of the expanse. Eliminate both of these, and then fly to the underside of the wing. Destroy the orange-marked turrets using your Repulsors and Unibeam attacks. After destroying several of the turrets on the wing underside, you should be finished with the objective.

When ready, float through the girders and ascend until you can see the hangar bay. If the hangar is open, then aim at the orange target marker and destroy the hangar. If not, then go back under the runway and hide amongst the girders until Jarvis announces that the hangar is open. The two hangars on one side of the fortress open, and then after a long interval, the two on the other side open.

## Destroy the Hangars

Jarvis warns that the hangars have opened. Fighter jets begin flying high above the fortress, seeking to pelt Iron Man with missiles. This makes the upper surface of the fortress a very dangerous place to hang out. Therefore, fly to the edge of a wing and ascend into the girder-filled area beneath one of the hangar runways. These nice little cocoons make it extremely difficult for the jet fighters' missiles to hit you.

## DANGEROUS EXHAUST!

The flames emanating from the fortress's engines may be more dangerous than you realize. Flying through the exhaust not only damages Iron Man, it can knock him several hundred yards away from the ship. If Iron Man ever travels too far from the ship during this mission, the fortress begins firing concussion grenades that make it nearly impossible to get back to the ship. This could result in mission failure!

## Shatter the Cooling Elements

When all four hangars are destroyed, Jarvis highlights four cooling structures on the undersides of the upper wings. Engage your afterburners and reroute power to your

thrusters. Fly over the upper surface of the wing, then descend before the front into the dark middle-space between the upper and lower wings. New weapons and soldiers in Maggia Prototype Battlesuits protect the two cooling structures on either side of the fortress. Eliminate

the opposition quickly, and then take out the cooling elements mounted to the underside of the upper wing.

When finished with one side of the fortress, engage thrusters and fly across the front of the fortress to the other side, and do the same. When all four cooling elements are destroyed, the hangar on the front of the central structure opens.

### SUIT WARS

**The guys in the Prototype Battlesuits are fun to grapple. Reroute power to melee, and give it a try to see what happens!**

## The Cooling Tank Bay

Fly to the center part in front of the ship, and hover outside the newly-opened cooling tank bay. Try to fly off center, so that Iron Man is only exposed to two of the turrets mounted inside the bay at a time. Destroy the visible turrets

before letting Iron Man naturally float into the bay thanks to wind resistance.

Land on the inner surface and move off to the side, so that most of the turrets inside the bay cannot target Iron Man. Destroy the nearest turrets, then move out to the corner of the nearest coolant tank and destroy the turrets visible at the far end. This should leave on a few more turrets to take out at the back of the bay.

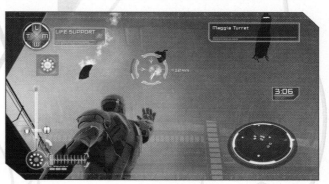

Destroying the turrets first is important, because with that done you can take all the time needed to destroy the four coolant tanks. The tanks themselves are durable, but defenseless without the turrets.

BASICS

ARMOR & UPGRADES

ENEMIES

MISSIONS

ONE MAN ARMY

SECRETS

SYS001    00 0098 230
SYS002    00 7802 102
SYS003    01 6730 250
SYS004    00 7349 221

SYS005    01 3462 21
SYS006    00 1423 11

BIO ACTIVE
VENT ACTIVE

XBOX 360 ▪ PS3

## The Exposed Reactor

Engage afterburners to fight wind resistance, and fly out of the coolant tank bay. Ascend to the upper surface of the central structure and fly toward the rear. As you approach the trench used to help take out the helipads

and missile turrets earlier, the massive hatch covering the main reactor slides open. Drop inside the reactor bay, and land on the surface.

The reactor is surrounded by more turrets than were in the last bay. Take out only the ones that have a clear shot at Iron Man from your side of the central reactor. Then fire up the Unibeam from less than 80m away, and pour on some missiles to destroy it and sink this big behemoth into the sea!

## MISSION WRAP-UP

### NEW TECH AVAILABLE

**CORE SYSTEMS UPGRADE (TECH LEVEL 3)**

**ADVANCED MARK III SYSTEM**

**ADVANCED STRIKER SYSTEM**

**SPECTER SYSTEM**

### SUIT CONFIGURATION: PRE-MISSION 07

If the Auxiliary Weapons upgrade is still lingering, please upgrade that rather than the Core Systems if funds are short. Otherwise, someone who has collected every available asset from all previous missions should be able to afford all previous upgrades plus the new Core system upgrade to Tech Level 3. If not, seriously consider replaying previous missions in the Mission Archive until you have the funs needed to make Iron Man as powerful as possible. The next mission is a doozy!

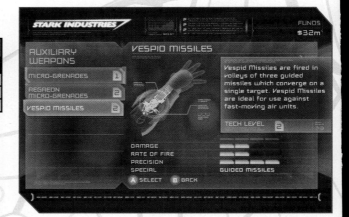

**STARK INDUSTRIES**    FUNDS $32m

**AUXILIARY WEAPONS**

MICRO-GRENADES   1

REGAEON MICRO-GRENADES   2

VESPID MISSILES   2

**VESPID MISSILES**

Vespid Missiles are fired in volleys of three guided missiles which converge on a single target. Vespid Missiles are ideal for use against fast-moving air units.

TECH LEVEL   2

DAMAGE
RATE OF FIRE
PRECISION
SPECIAL    GUIDED MISSILES

A SELECT   B BACK

BASICS

ARMOR & UPGRADES

ENEMIES

MISSIONS

ONE MAN ARMY

SECRETS

# 7 ARCTIC BATTLE

## MISSION DESCRIPTION

*Just when Tony Stark thinks his adventures as Iron Man have curbed the illegal use of Stark Industries technology, Air Force pilot Lt. Colonel Jim Rhodes drops by the office to request his help in preventing the takeover of a nuclear base in Russia by Advanced Idea Mechanics (AIM). Although Stark is hesitant to get involved, a quick check of his records indicates that AIM is the largest buyer of Stark weapons, and is therefore using them to usurp the balance of international political stability. Looks like Iron Man needs to dress warm...*

## PRIMARY OBJECTIVE

DEFEAT TITANIUM MAN.

ASSETS: 91

## HERO OBJECTIVES

PROTECT THE NUCLEAR FACILITY.

ASSETS: 20

## BONUS OBJECTIVES

TIME CHALLENGE: 12:00

ASSETS: 9

## ENEMIES

ENEMIES TO DESTROY: 72

ASSETS: 9

## *Piece by Piece*

Reroute power to thrusters and use afterburners to fly along the snow-covered canyon directly ahead of the starting point. Decelerate and reroute power to weapons when Jarvis announces that anti-air units are tracking you. As you emerge from the canyon, fly to the right and destroy a Merc SAM Battery positioned amid the small buildings there.

A convoy of tanks and SAM Batteries are rolling up the hill. Fly after them and use Repulsors and missiles to take out the convoy. They were headed for the nuclear plant just up the road and across the bridge. Navigate there and eliminate the gunship and SAM Batteries guarding the plant entrance, as well as the soldiers who come out a moment later.

## FIGHTING OCCASIONAL AIR SUPPORT

Attacking any of the Merc bases causes them to radio for air support. Two fighter jets appear as you eliminate the forces near the nuclear plant. Ascend as high as possible, face the Merc Fighters as they approach, dodge their missiles and then take them out with Repulsor fire. Rerouting power to your weapons helps destroy the fighters before they fly out of range. More fighters appear each time a base is attacked.

Reroute power to your thrusters and fly along the bottom of the gorge on a westbound heading until you reach the airbase. As you reach the edge of the mountains, reduce speed and reroute power to weapons. Use Unibeams to take out the gunships floating over the runway, then gradually hover toward the airfield at a low altitude. By this point, you need only destroy one or two more orange-marked targets before your objective changes. However, the latter parts of the mission become easier if you stick around and wipe out all forces in this area.

### Crush All Anti-Air

Iron Man must now take out the anti-air units in three separate locations. Scan the area for the location to the northeast where only two units are located, not far away. Fly there at low altitude to prevent SAM Batteries from firing, and begin destroying all the units. Although most of the enemies at this location are optional, the latter part of this mission becomes easier if you clear the area completely.

Fly south across the gorge and attack the larger installation, continuing to maintain a low altitude. Take out the gunship hovering over the area first, then saturate the area with missiles and Repulsor fire. As the enemy units dwindle, start using Unibeam attacks to finish off the remainders. More fighter jets should be targeting Iron Man from above, so ascend toward the clouds and take them out.

BASICS

ARMOR & UPGRADES

ENEMIES

MISSIONS

ONE MAN ARMY

SECRETS

## Enter Titanium Man

Reroute power to your thrusters and fly over to the nuclear plant. Siphoning radioactive power from the plant is the enigmatic Merc leader Bullski, who wears a titanium suit suspiciously similar to Iron Man's. Although Bullski has a target marker, he is invulnerable to harm while drawing power from the nuclear reactors.

As the dialog continues, preempt the incoming reinforcements by engaging afterburners and flying northeast. Land

at the first base you destroyed, and wait there until Bullski activates a massive nuclear powered laser named "Tatiana".

## Destroy Tatiana's Power Generators

If you flew to the first base location as previously recommended, then when Tatiana wakes up a SAM Battery emerges from the garage nearby. Quickly eliminate it with a fully charged Unibeam attack, then reroute power to your thrusters and fly northeast through the mountains.

An AIM Dropship is inbound for the base. Engage your afterburners and collide with the Dropship midair to damage it severely.

Then blow it up with another fully charged Unibeam attack before it can land and unload AIM Tanks or SAM Batteries.

Fly south to the next-closest base, and try to collide in midair with the Dropship attempting to land there. Finish off the Dropship, as well as SAM Battery that has appeared in this area.

Around this time, Jarvis finishes his analysis of the laser cannon's recharge system. The laser and its shield system are powered by three power stations, one located at each of the bases and at the airfield. Just before the laser fires, the top hatch of the generator opens and the generator rises through. When the generator is exposed, destroy it quickly with a combo of Missiles and Repulsor fire.

## SURVIVING TATIANA

**Throughout the following events, the giant laser repeatedly fires at Iron Man. If the laser hits, Iron Man's life support is reduced by roughly half. The laser fires every 15 to 30 seconds, and audibly warms up for at least 2 seconds before firing. If Iron Man takes a hit from the laser while fighting other enemies, the situation can become very dangerous rather quickly. All suit reboots should be saved until you face the boss at the end of the mission.**

**The key to surviving the laser is to fight at low altitudes, taking cover behind buildings and mountains if possible. Check your cover by using the Look control to rotate your camera view toward the nuclear plant where the laser is located. If you can see the laser, it can target you. Avoid leaving valid cover locations until just after you hear the laser fire.**

**The laser can also be used to eliminate enemies more easily. Simply hover to the opposite side of an enemy unit, so that they fall between Iron Man and the giant laser. When the laser fires, the enemy takes the brunt of the damage. Be advised that the laser may penetrate the enemy and damage Iron Man as well.**

Fly northeast back towards the first base, and start attacking the Dropship and enemy units that have landed there since your last visit. The Dropship also deploys AIM Hover Soldiers, who fly around like Iron Man and attack with handheld proton lasers. These foes are particularly pesky, and can drive Iron Man's life support down quickly. Hover low in the chasm where the giant laser cannot hit you, and destroy these enemies as they appear at the cliff's edge above.

As the base clears up, wait for the laser to fire and then quickly fly behind the power station. Hold your ground against more reinforcements, and wait for the generator to emerge from the top of the station. Destroy it as soon as possible.

Descend to the bottom of the gorge that divides the center of the area, and fly along the bottom toward the airfield. Reroute power to your weapons as you approach, and start attacking the enemy reinforcements that have retaken the area. The Dropships have a tendency to move ahead of the units they drop, serving to draw your fire away from them. Try to ignore the Dropships by flying past them, and destroy them last.

After clearing the airfield significantly enough, fly behind the power station in this area, and destroy the generators as they emerge from the top of the power station.

## Destroy Tatiana

When all three power stations that charge Tatiana's laser and shields are destroyed, the cannon is exposed and can finally be annihilated. Reroute power to your thrusters and use your afterburners to fly back to the laser cannon as quickly and directly as possible. Bullski aims the laser cannon at the nuclear reactor. Iron Man has one minute to destroy the laser cannon before it damages the reactor enough to breech the core, causing a dangerous meltdown that will endanger the population. Failure to protect the nuclear facility from harm reduces the assets awarded at the end of the mission.

Although new AIM Tanks and Gunships appear around the laser cannon, try to ignore them and fly behind the laser. Target the base of the cannon and hit with missiles and Unibeam attacks to bring it down quickly.

Land on the ground in the small area directly behind the cannon. Run around the area and target the AIM Gunships directly overhead, plus any Dropships or Hover Soldiers that come into view. Then hover at a low altitude and destroy the two AIM Tanks in front of the cannon. When all other enemy units are clear, reroute power to your weapons and start flying toward the nuclear plant for your showdown against Titanium Man.

BIO  ACTIVE
VENT  ACTIVE
RESP  FLTR ACTIVE
OPTIC  ACTIVE

CYBERNET
ROOT: 384578
.../09: 29058

PART GEN
ROOT: 3842532372 030
.../03: 290783

BOOT JET: 23%

771  DL

UNI BEAM: 49%

003  OMR

REP BEAM:

675 %

SPEED
TNC.......................32%
PLPT......................
PLPT......................

TEMP
ODS.......................92%
FAN.......................88%
SMO.......................28%

LIFE SUPPORT
TYK.......................12%

BASICS

ARMOR & UPGRADES

ENEMIES

MISSIONS

ONE MAN ARMY

SECRETS

# TITANIUM MAN

**1** Titanium Man is an extremely resilient enemy who can regenerate his life throughout the battle. Therefore, the first priority is to take out the AIM Missile Hover Soldiers emerging from the nearby barracks. Fly around the south side of the nuclear plant to make them easier to target versus Titanium Man. Use missiles and Repulsor fire to take them out quickly. A second set of Missile Hover Soldiers emerge from the barracks to reinforce the area. Take them out also, so that you are free to face Titanium Man, mano a mano. More Hover Soldiers may appear, but there's time enough between each wave for you to take Titanium Man down a notch.

**2** If your life support is reduced to the point where it begins flashing red, quickly engage afterburners and fly to the bottom of the nearby gorge. Hide under the bridge, where Titanium Man will not follow. Reroute power to life support to regenerate health more quickly. Then reroute power back to your weapons and fly out of the gorge to continue fighting Titanium Man.

**3** Titanium Man's most devastating attack is a close-quarters grapple that is a bit difficult to avoid and reduces Iron Man's life support by almost half. To avoid this, remain at 100-150 meters from him at all times. This range also helps to avoid or dodge Titanium Man's midair ramming attacks. Pelt him continuously with auxiliary and main weapons until the battle is won. If you're unfortunate enough to get

within range of Titanium Man's charge attack, hit the Grapple button when he charges in to turn the tables and throw him instead. This is a timing mini-game, but if done correctly, it can definitely save your hide.

**4** Occasionally, Titanium Man begins glowing green. This means he is charging up a radioactive Unibeam attack. You must remain within 100-150 meters of him so that you can clearly see him preparing this attack. Press the Dodge button at the instant he fires his Unibeam, and Iron Man takes no damage. Another way to avoid this attack is to fly for cover behind one of the nuclear reactors. Otherwise, this attack reduces life support by at least half. Right after Titanium Man fires a Unibeam and misses, quickly hit him with a Unibeam of your own.

**5** When Titanium Man's health is reduced to half, or at certain time intervals throughout the battle, he breaks off attacking and begins flying around his recharging post at the center of the nuclear plant. Just before he settles onto the recharge pad, hit him with a Unibeam from a range of 50-100 meters. A direct hit knocks him to the ground, and he must recuperate before returning to his usual flight pattern. Hit him while he's down with Missiles and another Unibeam, if you have it in you. If Titanium Man manages to settle on the recharge platform, he can regenerate more than half his life support. This is a hard and long battle, but continue attacking him until the battle is won!

## MISSION WRAP-UP

| NEW TECH AVAILABLE |
|---|
| **POWER SYSTEMS UPGRADE (TECH LEVEL 3)** |
| PLASMA CORE |
| HEC AUGMENTED |
| **MOBILITY ENHANCEMENTS UPGRADE (TECH LEVEL 3)** |
| AEQUO THRUSTERS |
| CELERITAS THRUSTERS |
| AGILITAS THRUSTERS |

## SUIT CONFIGURATION: PRE-MISSION 08

Power level is critical to Iron Man's combat prowess, as you've certainly learned by getting this far. Therefore, upgrade the Power Systems to Tech Level 3 for $121 million. Equip either of the new level 3 power modules. If funds are deficient, replay Mission 07 to achieve all assets available, and financing should be no problem.

# 8 LOST DESTROYER

## MISSION DESCRIPTION

*Rhodey informs Tony that a prototype naval destroyer fitted with advanced Stark weaponry has gone missing. The Lt. Colonel suspects the involvement of AIM. It's up to Iron Man to eliminate AIM forces congregating around the destroyer and recover the ship without endangering the crew.*

## PRIMARY OBJECTIVE

DEFEAT AIM AND SECURE THE DESTROYER.

ASSETS: 94

## HERO OBJECTIVE

AVOID HARMING THE DESTROYER AND ITS CREW.

ASSETS: 22

## BONUS OBJECTIVES

TIME CHALLENGE: 14:00

ASSETS: 9

## ENEMIES TO DESTROY

ENEMIES TO DESTROY: 108

ASSETS: 9

## *Eliminate Base Defenses*

Iron Man must destroy the enemies surrounding the four bases in the region. The area directly in front of the starting position is heavily guarded by AIM forces. Use the snowy hills as cover when needed while destroying the enemy units. The AIM Gunships are particularly devastating opponents, and should be prioritized as targets. More gunships fly into the area when the first set are brought down in flames.

When the number of enemies is greatly reduced, begin hovering inward at a low altitude. Avoid directly approaching the area surrounding the ship, which is sealed off by a shimmering force field. Entering the force field causes Iron Man's systems to scramble, disabling his vision and weaponry. Fly out of the area as quickly as possible if you enter it by accident.

The distortion zone around the tanker is powered by a Controller Device that sits on the ground behind the small building off to the right. Hover along the right side of the area, and destroy the drone to eliminate the distortion field. Then continue eliminating enemies marked with orange targets until Jarvis notifies you that three bases remain.

# THE CONTROLLER SUBMARINE

The Controller Submarine which is the stage boss breaks through the ice to surface in several locations, always near to Iron Man, prior to the boss fight proper. The sub is an optional target, since it cannot be destroyed until the actual battle. The submarine submerges again after a minute or two. If the sub emerges in an area where other enemies are still present, the cannon on the front end of the sub can make survival difficult. If this is the case, target the sub's cannon and fire Missiles and Unibeams at it until it quits firing. The sub still reappears within a minute or two, but this should give you enough time to reduce the number of other enemies in the area. Otherwise, avoid wasting time or missiles on the Controller Submarine until the actual boss fight.

## The Second Base

After eliminating the base defenses near the starting point, fly low over the mountains to the north to reach the next-closest base, a shipping dock frozen over with ice. Eliminate the AA Turrets on the closest hill, then fly low to the hill and use it as cover while wiping out the other forces.

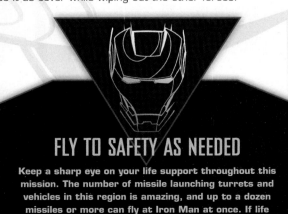

# FLY TO SAFETY AS NEEDED

Keep a sharp eye on your life support throughout this mission. The number of missile launching turrets and vehicles in this region is amazing, and up to a dozen missiles or more can fly at Iron Man at once. If life support begins flashing, use afterburners to fly behind a hill as quickly as possible. Wait there until Iron Man's life and energy recoup, and then return to battle.

The Controller Device generating the distortion field in this area rests on the ice floor, tucked in the inside corner of the dock. Destroy it immediately so that you may land or hover low to the surface, and thereby draw less fire from anti-aircraft weapons. The submarine also surfaces in this area, but try to ignore it and keep eliminating targets with orange markers until Jarvis says its okay to move on.

## Base Number Three

When finished at the sea dock area, fly north again to find the third base. Hover at low altitude and gradually float into the base, eliminating the nearest enemies as you proceed. Many missile turrets and SAM Batteries located in this area make it critical to stay out of the air in this zone.

Fly to the south side of the base outside the distortion zone in order to target the Controller Device propagating the field. The device is positioned on a low platform on the side of the building. When the field is destroyed, land on the ground inside the base and destroy the remaining weapons in the area.

## The Multi-Level Base

The last base is located to the southeast, and due to its sprawl it might just be the hardest base to bring down. Descend low to the ice and gradually eliminate the ground level units. Watch out for the mobile flak guns that roll in from the northeast while you attack the base. The howitzers and SAM Batteries on the bridge high above can also be troubling. The Controller Sub emerges from the ice, occasionally. Destroy the gun on the front end if needed, but focus mainly on eliminating the forces on the lake level of the last base.

When the lower area is clear or at least mostly clear, fly around to the farthest side of the distortion zone, eliminating gunships flying around the area. The Controller Device creating the distortion field in this area is located behind the central building on the upper plane. Destroy it to remove the field, and then targeting and eliminating the rest of the unit should be easier.

# CONTROLLER SUBMARINE

**1** The Controller Submarine begins surfacing in the area surrounding the captured prototype destroyer to the far north. The Controller is exerting some kind of mind control on the crew, which cause them to fire on Iron Man. In order to achieve the maximum amount of assets for this mission, you must avoid hitting any of the targets on the destroyer. If you do not care about getting the most assets possible, then destroy the Controller Device on the rear deck of the sub and take out all the destroyer's missile platforms. Doing so makes this battle much easier.

**2** To destroy the Controller Submarine without damaging the destroyer, land on the ice behind the Controller Sub when it surfaces. Use Unibeams and Missiles repeatedly to take out the front cannon of the sub, and then attack the orange target on the center of its body with the same attacks. Watch your fire and listen to Jarvis, and avoid attacking when the submerges to reduce the chances of accidentally hitting the destroyer. Use your mini-radar to determine where the sub is about to surface next, and be there to meet it.

**3** If energy or life support run low, fly away to a safe distance and dodge missiles from the destroyer until Iron Man fully recuperates, then return to battle. Keep attacking the sub until it sinks into the ocean permanently.

## MISSION WRAP-UP

| NEW TECH AVAILABLE |
| --- |
| **REPULSORS UPGRADE (TECH LEVEL 3)** |
| **ADVANCED ION REPULSOR** |
| **MESON CANNON REPULSOR** |
| **MULTI-PHASE GATLING REPULSOR** |

## SUIT CONFIGURATION: PRE-MISSION 09

Upgrading the Repulsors system to Tech Level 3 is just the ticket for the next mission. Since Mission 09 is another long battle against Titanium Man, rate of fire will be important. Equip either the Advanced Ion Repulsor or the Multi-phase Gatling Repulsor to help win the battle more efficiently.

# 9 ON DEFENSE

BASICS

ARMOR & UPGRADES

ENEMIES

MISSIONS

ONE MAN ARMY

SECRETS

## MISSION DESCRIPTION

*While trying to uncover AIM's main objective, Iron Man is called out on his home turf when Titanium Man and AIM attack the Stark Industries building in Long Beach. Clearly, it seems that Iron Man must eliminate Titanium Man or face his own extinction.*

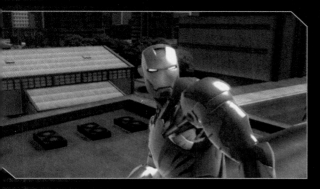

## PRIMARY OBJECTIVE

DEFEAT TITANIUM MAN.

ASSETS: 100

## HERO OBJECTIVES

AVOID DISRUPTING THE CITY'S POWER SUPPLY.

ASSETS: 4 (X5.5)

## BONUS OBJECTIVES

TIME CHALLENGE: 11:00

ASSETS: 10

## ENEMIES

ENEMIES TO DESTROY: 35

ASSETS: 10

# TITANIUM MAN

**1** Surviving the first few seconds of the battle is tough. Titanium Man is just ten feet away, and usually starts the battle with a grapple attack that knocks Iron Man's life support down to half or less. Couple this with the other problem, that the Stark Industries building is surrounded by AIM tanks firing a constant barrage of photon beams, and most likely experience you will experience a suit failure within the first few seconds. Take advantage of this initial failure, since enemies do not resume attacking Iron Man for a few seconds after a system reboot. Use the opportunity to fly behind one of the nearby buildings, and use for cover. Move out from cover to attack Titanium Man with Repulsors and Vespid Missiles, and then fly back behind cover when he tries to perform his own version of the Unibeam.

**2** Continue attacking Titanium Man until he begins to fly away. He heads for one of four power substations at the outskirts of the city. There, he grasps the Tesla converters and recharges his suit, regaining a small amount of his life. As Jarvis explains, destroying these power substations prevents Titanium Man from regaining lost life. However, without power, the citizens of Long Beach become vulnerable to attack. Destroying any of the power substations causes failure of the Hero Objective for this mission.

Boss Fight continued on next page >

230
102
250
221

02 210
423 11

XBOX 360 • PS3

VENT ACTIVE

# TITANIUM MAN

**3** In order to defeat Titanium Man and also achieve the Hero Objective, avoid attacking him while he is recharging. Instead, destroy any AIM Tanks or Hover soldiers in the area, or grapple the Hover soldiers to regain lost life support. As Titanium Man finishes revitalizing himself, grapple one of the nearby SAM Batteries and fire at Titanium Man. Using the SAM Battery reduces Titanium Man's health by large amounts. The rest of the battle then becomes much easier. Again, don't forget to hit the Grapple button if Titanium Man attempts to charge and grapple with you.

**4** Between recharges, Titanium Man flies back to the center of town near Stark Industries. As before, fly low and take cover behind a building, somewhere that none or few of the surrounding AIM Tanks can inflict additional damage to Iron Man. Slip out from cover occasionally to hit Titanium Man with Repulsors/Vespid Missile combos, then retreat to cover. In the event Titanium Man moves in to flush Iron Man out of

cover, activate energy shield countermeasures and fly to a new location, taking cover behind a building. Then deactivate the energy shields and resume your previous strategy. Pursue him on his way to another power station, destroy AIM units in the area and grapple SAM Batteries to use against Titanium Man. Honestly, when using the SAM Battery grapple against Titanium Man just after he recharges, the battle shouldn't last much longer than his first recharge.

## LET HIM LINGER

This boss fight mission may take a few tries to clear, but don't let it become overly frustrating. The most difficult aspect is attempting to destroy 35 enemies before taking out Titanium Man to achieve the bonus objective. This requires you to make Titanium Man your secondary focus, while you grapple AIM Tanks and take out enemies surrounding all of the power substations.

**771** DLP

UNI BEAM: 49% IIIII I I I  II II

**003** OMP

REP BEAM: IIIII IIIII

## MISSION WRAP-UP

**675**

| NEW TECH AVAILABLE |
| --- |
| AUXILIARY WEAPONS UPGRADE |
| GYGES MICRO-GRENADES |
| ADVANCED VESPID MISSILES |

SPEED
TNC.................... 2%
PLPT.................... 78%
PLPT.................... 78%

### SUIT CONFIGURATION: PRE-MISSION 10

TEMP
ODS..............
FAN..............
SMO..............

If reduced to a choice between upgrading Power Systems or Auxiliary Weapons to Tech Level 3, definitely go with the Power Systems upgrade. Power should be routed to your weapons systems throughout most of Mission 10, upgrading the Power System means that Tech Level 3 Repulsors can be fired more often with less energy drain. By completing Mission 10, you should be able to obtain the last upgrade to Auxiliary Weapons. Also, be sure to equip the Multi-phase Gatling Repulsor module for greater ease in completing Mission 10.

LIFE SUPP
TYK.......................... 12%

BASICS

ARMOR & UPGRADES

ENEMIES

MISSIONS

ONE MAN ARMY

SECRETS

# 10 SAVE PEPPER

## MISSION DESCRIPTION

*With Pepper's kidnapping, it becomes clear that Titanium Man's attack was merely a diversion. Compounding the situation is Obadiah Stane's admittance that he is behind AIM's buildup and recent improvements in implementing Stark Industries technology. But Tony can do nothing about Stane at the moment, since rescuing Pepper from AIM is his chief objective. As Iron Man, he flies to where AIM is holding Pepper captive; a research station with an active nuclear reactor. With Iron Man in the vicinity, AIM intends to destroy the reactor and cause a thermonuclear explosion to kill Iron Man and Pepper with certainty. The main objective of the mission is to prevent AIM from causing the reactor explosion.*

## PRIMARY OBJECTIVE

PREVENT REACTOR DESTRUCTION WHILE PEPPER IS INSIDE.

ASSETS: 103

## HERO OBJECTIVES

PROTECT THE OUTLYING OCCUPIED BUILDINGS.

ASSETS: 24

## BONUS OBJECTIVES

TIME CHALLENGE: 25:00

ASSETS: 10

## ENEMIES

ENEMIES TO DESTROY: 85

ASSETS: 10

## An Obvious Trap

The reactor is surrounded by four Tesla converter towers. At the top of each Tesla tower is an upright energy ring. Flying through the ring causes the Tesla towers to form an electromagnetic barrier around the main reactor. Anything except Iron Man that falls inside this barrier

is immediately destroyed. For instance, start the mission by flying through one of the rings at the top of one of the Tesla towers. The initial forces surrounding the reactor are swiftly eliminated. Unfortunately, the Tesla towers need several minutes to recharge before another electromagnetic barrier can be erected around the reactor. Using the Tesla towers wisely at just the right moments is the key ingredient to survival throughout this mission.

## Incoming Missiles

AIM launches clusters of long range ICBM missiles at the reactor. Hover over the inland wall of the reactor and scan the horizon for incoming missile clusters. When a swarm of missiles start coming in, use your Repulsors to destroy them before they hit the reactor. Although the clusters may appear to be a long stream, they actually come in waves from two directions. While hovering over the reactor, destroy the missiles coming in from the left, and then the clusters flying in from the right. Go back and forth destroying the missiles coming from either side until Jarvis announces that the Tesla towers are back online. Then quickly fly through the nearest Tesla ring to erect another electromagnetic barrier around the reactor, protecting it from the rest of the missiles and simultaneously destroying all recently arriving gunships in the reactor vicinity. For the rest of the mission, watch your radar for incoming missile attacks.

SYS005    01 3462 2109867 990
SYS006    00 1423 1122496 002

BIO ACTIVE
VENT ACTI
RESP FLTR
OPTIC ACT

||||||||||    |||||||||

CYBERNET
ROOT: 384578
../09: 29058

PART GEN
ROOT: 384253
../03: 29078

## PATROL THE OUTLYING TOWERS!

Just because a tower is marked with yellow on the radar doesn't mean it isn't under light attack. As is especially the case with the tower nearest the beachfront, gunships can hover around a tower and attack it repeatedly without the tower being marked with a yellow dot on your radar. This means you cannot rely solely on the radar to save your hide. Keep a constant eye on all towers by hovering above the reactor throughout the mission, and clear the area around all the towers whenever needed. Keep in mind that the easiest way to eliminate gunships is with a midair grapple!

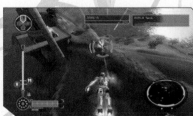

## Protect the Towers

BOOT JET:23%
When the first wave of missiles is destroyed, AIM changes tactics. Dropships begin leaving Tanks near the Tesla towers surrounding the area. The tanks begin attacking the towers. Towers under siege are marked with yellow dots on the
771 DLP
radar. When a tower is in trouble, quickly fly to its location and destroy any tanks, howitzers and gunships in the vicinity.
UNI BEAM:49%
When the tower's dot on the radar changes from yellow back to green, the tower is safe. While protecting the towers, fly
003 OMP
through the Telsa hoops whenever possible to destroy any gunships that may be attacking the reactor while you're away.

REP BEAM: ||||
Prevent at least one of the Tesla towers
675 %
from being destroyed in order to achieve the Hero Objective for this mission.

SPEED
TNC.....................32%
PLPT...............
PLPT...............

## Combined Assault!

Things get truly hairy as more missiles start flying in from various directions while ground forces attack the outlying towers. The best strategy is to stick to destroying the forces near the towers, and trigger the electromagnetic field around the reactor whenever possible. Use Vespid Missiles and Unibeams to clean up the ground forces attacking the towers as quickly as possible, then hightail it back to the reactor and fry the incoming missiles with Repulsors.

Taking a stationary position at this point in the mission is not a wise idea. Fly between the towers, and destroy incoming missiles clusters while flying from one endangered tower to the next.

TEMP
ODS...............
FAN...............
SMO...............

LIFE SUPPORT
TYK...............12%

BASICS

ARMOR & UPGRADES

ENEMIES

MISSIONS

ONE MAN ARMY

SECRETS

## Shockwave!

Protect the Tesla towers to the best of your abilities until the final assault wave, which commences when missiles begin pouring in from multiple directions in wider spread patterns, all at once. Fly through the Tesla tower immediately, then use afterburners to quickly fly above the reactor. The electromagnetic field takes out most but not all of them. While hovering over the reactor, shoot down several dozens of the missiles coming in from the southeast, then eliminate some of the ones coming from the southwest. As soon as the Tesla towers are ready again, fly through one of the rings again to erect the electromagnetic barrier one last time. If successful, this should be enough to eliminate the remaining gunships and protect the reactor from the remaining missiles in flight.

Spend the rest of the mission eliminating the remaining ground forces to ensure achieving the Hero Objective.

## MISSION WRAP-UP

### NEW TECH AVAILABLE
N/A

### SUIT CONFIGURATION: PRE-MISSION 11

Complete upgrades to the Mark III suit by purchasing the Auxiliary Weapons upgrade for $125 million. We strongly recommend equipping the Advanced Vespid Missiles module for the remaining missions, since they home in on targets at long distances.

098 230
02 102
0 250
22

S
SY

BIO
VENT

# 11 ISLAND MELTDOWN

## MISSION DESCRIPTION

*Although Stane is behind all that has transpired, Iron Man must eliminate the threat AIM poses. Learning the location of a powerful proton cannon that AIM intends to turn against the populace, Iron Man races to the cannon's location among a series of Mediterranean islands near Greece. There, Iron Man encounters a massive defense force protecting a network of bases that provide power to the central proton cannon. Iron Man must disable each of the cannon's power couplings at the outlying bases, and then destroy the cannon itself.*

## PRIMARY OBJECTIVE

DESTROY THE PROTON CANNON.

ASSETS: 105

## HERO OBJECTIVE

PREVENT CANNON ATTACKS ON CIVILIAN TARGETS.

ASSETS: 4 (X6)

## BONUS OBJECTIVES

TIME CHALLENGE: 12:00

ASSETS: 11

## ENEMIES TO DESTROY

ENEMIES TO DESTROY: 80

ASSETS: 11

## The East Power Coupling

From Iron Man's starting point, fly directly ahead at low altitude across the water's surface, heading northwest. Hover roughly 250 meters away from the east base, and use Repulsors and Vespid Missiles to destroy the AIM-X defenses on the platform. Use the low hills as cover to reduce damage, and to duck behind when gunships fly onto the scene.

As you clear out the sky and the nearest portion of the base platform, hover inward and continue dismantling armaments. If your life support flashes red, drop below the base platform to recuperate. Enemies throughout this stage reappear after short absences, so do not waste time destroying them all. Eliminate only enough to give yourself a clear shot at the orange-marked power coupling. Destroy it and fly north to the farthest base.

BASICS

ARMOR & UPGRADES

ENEMIES

MISSIONS

ONE MAN ARMY

SECRETS

## COUNTERCLOCKWISE ASSAULT

The mission becomes slightly easier if you move from base to base around the islands in a counterclockwise fashion. Destroy the power coupling at each base, and then quickly fly in a counterclockwise circle to the next target. Do not linger too long at one base, because the enemies can restore the power couplings!

## CANNON SHOT!

Grapple several outlying howitzers near this base, and turn them on their fellow AIM units to really do some damage. Howitzers fire mortar shells straight up in the air, which then fall on targets a few seconds later. But instant gratification isn't the name of the game with howitzers; the damage the inflict is so powerful, it's worth the wait!

## North Power Coupling

Proceeding in a counterclockwise fashion around the island ring, fly toward the base at the north end of the stage. Approach the base from a low altitude from the southeast, taking out ground opposition and gunships as you make your way inward. After eliminating all armored anti-air units on the nearest side of the platform, target the orange-marked power coupling and destroy it with barrages of Vespid Missiles and Unibeam attacks.

## South Power Coupling

Having flown almost full-circle around the islands by now, you come to the most heavily-defended base. By approaching at a low altitude from the west, you can take cover behind some rocks roughly 250 meters away from the base. Eliminate soldiers hovering in AIM Battlesuits and gunships that await your arrival. Stay low enough that only the bottom cannons and turrets on the base can target you. When those are destroyed, target the power coupling and destroy it. Probably not much time remains before the first power coupling is restored, so pour all of your power into it!

## West Power Coupling

Watch out for hovering AIM-X soldiers as you attack the base where the western power coupling for the cannon is located. The ones in this area like to fly behind Iron Man and ambush him continually from different altitudes. As with all the other bases, gradually blast your way in until you have a clear shot at the power coupling, then saturate it with your most powerful attacks.

## AVOIDING BOMBARDMENT

Dropping into the water is an effective way to dodge missiles, if energy is low or chaff modules are not equipped.

# THE MELTER

**1** Do not worry about defeating Bruno Horgan - The Melter - because direct confrontation is entirely unnecessary. Fly toward the central island until Horgan emerges on the proton cannon's platform. Ignore the urge to fly into battle against him, since the central island is the most heavily-defended area in the mission. Instead, approach the central island from a low altitude, just above the ocean's surface. From the base of the cliffs outside the island, fire on the central proton cannon, which is marked with yellow. Stay within 250 meters, so that Repulsors and Unibeams remain effective against the cannon. Attack the cannon continuously until it explodes, killing Horgan in the blast.

**2** Hover soldiers and gunships fly into range as you attack the cannon, attempting to thwart your objective. Eliminate them quickly with Repulsor and missile combos, and then resume attacking the proton cannon. Watch the mini-radar for incoming missiles, and activate energy shields or dodge as necessary. Also watch the radar for aerial targets such as gunships and Battlesuit soldiers that may hover at long range behind Iron Man and ambush him continuously. Knock out these foes, and resume assaulting the cannon. Remember that hover soldiers can be grappled to recover life support more quickly, and take advantage of this if any of them move too close.

## HERO OBJECTIVE

To achieve this objective, clear out the defenses around Horgan as quickly as possible. Fly up to the proton cannon and wait for him to start charging. (The purple sphere is your cue.)

Dodge out of the way and force him to shoot where you were! His charged shot inflicts 50% damage to the cannon. Repeat this tactic twice and the cannon is no more!

BASICS

ARMOR & UPGRADES

ENEMIES

MISSIONS

ONE MAN ARMY

SECRETS

# 12 SPACE TETHER

## MISSION DESCRIPTION

*Iron Man's encounter with Horgan yields the information he has been seeking: AIM-X is powering their technology by drawing energy from an orbital satellite. By severing the space tether, Iron Man can nullify AIM-X's ability to wage war and subjugate the planet. And with AIM-X down for the count, Iron Man can finally turn his attention back to Stark Industries and Obadiah Stane's hostile takeover attempt.*

## PRIMARY OBJECTIVE

DISABLE THE SPACE TETHER.

ASSETS: 114

## HERO OBJECTIVES

SEVER THE TETHER BEFORE THE SATELLITE OVERLOADS.

ASSETS: 26

## BONUS OBJECTIVES

TIME CHALLENGE: 10:00

ASSETS: 11

## ENEMIES

ENEMIES TO DESTROY: 55

ASSETS: 11

## Destroy the MASER Accumulators

The space tether lies at the center of a massive meteor crater, and is protected by a MASER shield. The outer shield must be deactivated so that Iron Man can approach the tether and disable its control centers. The shield is powered by three MASER Accumulators at the far ends of the crater. By destroying the fuel cells beneath the accumulators, Iron Man can wipe them out and bring down the tether's defenses.

Fly toward the edge of the crater, taking out hovering soldiers in Battlesuits and gunships as you approach. Follow the pipeline that leads toward a small base built on the inside edge of the crater. Use this base as cover while destroying the armored defenses surrounding the first MASER Accumulator, located at the bottom of the crater far below. Additional forces approach from other bases at the far ends of the area, so do not waste time destroying absolutely every enemy target in the area.

SYS005    01 3462 2109867 990
SYS006    00 1423 1122496 002

BIO   ACTIVE
VENT  ACTIVE
RESP  FLTR  ACTIVE
OPTIC  ACTIVE

||||||||    ||||||||||    |||||||| || ||| |

CYBERNET  2 4587 800-ARM
ROOT: 3845782372 050
.../09: 290582394 503

PART GEN
ROOT: 384253
.../03: 290783

BOOT JET:23%

771 DLP

UNI BEAM:49%

003 OM

REP BEAM: ||||

675 %

SPEED
TNC............
PLPT............
PLPT............

TEMP
ODS............
FAN............
SMO............

LIFE SUPPORT
TYK..................12%

When the zone is fairly clear enough that Iron Man can survive the attacks of those few that remain, then land on the crater floor next to the MASER Accumulator and destroy the orange-marked fuel cells hanging below the device.

Ignore forces remaining in the area, and use afterburners to reach the next MASER Accumulator quickly. As before, eliminate only enough enemies to make the area safer, and then move beneath the Accumulator and destroy the fuel cells. Continue flying around the outer edge of the crater, and destroy the remaining two MASER Accumulators in the same fashion.

## Annihilate the Control Centers

With the tether's outer defenses removed, Iron Man can now fly toward the center. Four control centers mounted high up on the massive steel walls arranged around the tether must be destroyed in order to deactivate the inner shield system surrounding the base of the core. Each control center is marked in orange, and each can be disabled by destroying its radio control tower.

Pursue this objective quickly, without much concern for enemies in the surrounding area. Keep an eye on life support as you work, and use

afterburners to escape to a safe distance if your gauge begins flashing red.

## Cut Off the Power

Aware of Iron Man's progress, AIM-X attempts to overload and detonate the satellite. If the low orbital is destroyed, the nearby population suffers heavy casualties. Iron Man has 4 minutes to sever the power tether and prevent the overload in order to complete the Hero Objective.

BASICS

ARMOR & UPGRADES

ENEMIES

MISSIONS

ONE MAN ARMY

SECRETS

With the shield surrounding the tether's base deactivated, fly to the center and quickly destroy the massive power cables running from the exterior units to the tether's core. There are 16 of these cables surrounding the core. You must destroy at least half of them before the shield surrounding the tether connection becomes weak enough for Iron Man's weaponry to penetrate.

## Remove the Tether Supports

When enough power cables surrounding the base have been severed, the Tether Supports at the very top of the tower become highlighted with yellow markers. Quickly *fly*, do not hover, toward the top of the tower high above. Assault the Tether Supports with everything you've got, until the connectors explode and the tether cable flies up out of sight.

As you fight to sever the power cables, flying soldiers in Battlesuits hover at the upper edges of the tether behind you, attacking from above. Each time you relocate to another side of the tether base, take out most of these enemies before resuming your attack on the power cables. Otherwise, the damage suffered is too much to bear.

## MISSION WRAP-UP

### SUIT CONFIGURATION: PRE-SHOWDOWN

Configure your suit for the final mission by equipping the Advanced Striker System Core module, your preference of either the Advanced Ion Repulsor module or the Multiphase Gatling Repulsor module, and the Advanced Vespid Missiles. These modules provide the best offense against the final boss. Equip Tech Level 3 modules in all other systems to suit your playing preferences.

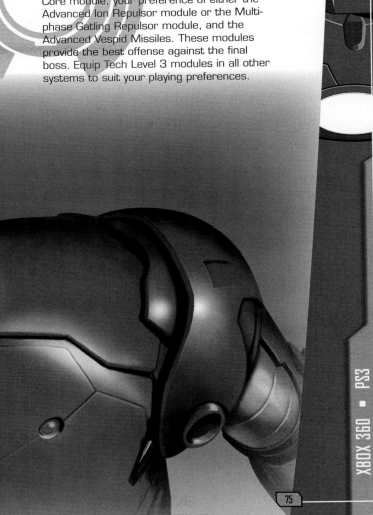

# 13 SHOWDOWN

## MISSION DESCRIPTION

*After annihilating Obadiah Stane's army built with pirated Stark technology, Iron Man returns to Long Beach to confront his former associate at his corporate headquarters building. But while Iron Man has been diverted by AIM-X forces, Stane has been preparing a little treat for Iron Man: the Iron Monger armor suit!*

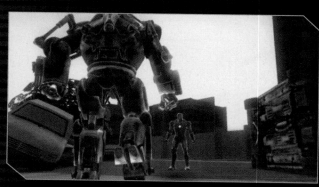

## PRIMARY OBJECTIVE

DEFEAT IRON MONGER.

ASSETS: 154

## HERO OBJECTIVE

DESTROY THE POWER REGULATORS.

ASSETS: 46

## BONUS OBJECTIVES

TIME CHALLENGE: 4:50

ASSETS: 10

## ENEMIES

ENEMIES TO DESTROY: 1

ASSETS: 10

# IRON MONGER

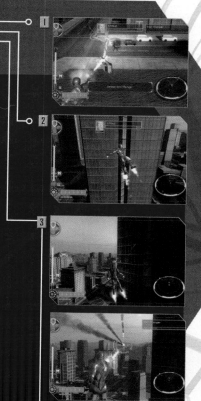

**1** Iron Man is too close for comfort at the start of the battle. Avoid the temptation to inflict immediate damage to Iron Monger. Instead, turn and fly away at least 100 meters, and take cover behind low buildings and walls. Any of Iron Monger's attacks, whether it be even his missile salvos or Repulsor fire, can drain Iron Man's life support completely within just a second. This is the most powerful enemy encountered in the game, and you must treat him as such every second or suffer the consequences.

**2** Flying from cover to cover, make your way over to the Stark Industries skyscraper at the center of the stage. Iron Monger finally ascends to your level when you hide behind this building. At this point, it is safe for you to ascend in altitude as well. However, you must hover on the opposite side of the building from Iron Monger.

**3** Once you position a building between you and Iron Monger, pursue a singular strategy for the rest of the battle: hover out beyond the corner to strike Iron Monger with a missile salvo and Repulsor fire, and then retreat behind the building corner before he counterattacks. Be sure to hover outward far enough that all Vespid Missiles home in on Iron Monger, and do not collide with the building instead. If you move out from the corner and happen to see Iron Monger firing his Repulsors or charging up a Unibeam attack, break off your attack and instead dodge back behind the building before suffering too much damage. Watch your radar, and move out from the corner to attack only after Iron Monger delivers a payload of missiles into the far side of the building. Repeat this strategy until notified otherwise by Jarvis.

Boss Fight continued on next page >

# IRON MONGER

BASICS

ARMOR & UPGRADES

ENEMIES

MISSIONS

ONE MAN ARMY

SECRETS

**4** Iron Monger also fires homing missiles that shoot straight up into the air and target Iron Man. These missiles cut Iron Man's life support by three quarters. The best way to avoid these missiles is by sticking close to the side of the building that you hide behind, so that the missile detonates on the rooftop or overshoots and hits the ground below. However, if you're quick and manage to time your grab, you can snatch the missile out of the air and return it to Iron Monger. This inflicts huge damage and can really make this fight easier.

**5** Occasionally, Iron Monger may flush you out of hiding by flying after you. If this happens, activate energy shields to prevent suit failure, and fly behind the next-closest corner of the same building. Then deactivate energy shields and resume the cat and mouse game using the building corners.

**6** Each time Iron Monger's life support empties, he drops to the ground momentarily. Saturate him with Vespid missiles, Unibeam attacks and Repulsor fire. As he gets up and flies to a new coordinate on the map, pursue him and continue firing Repulsors and missiles all the way. With good pursuit tactics, you should be able to knock off at least a third of his health before he stops and turns around to fight. When Iron Monger stops flying and turns to attack, immediately engage your energy shields and fly behind the nearest building. You can then resume your cat and mouse game using the building corners to knock down his next health bar.

**7** After emptying Iron Monger's life bar three times, he flies back to the starting point amid the lowest buildings of the stage. He stands on the ground and attacks as before. Hover behind one of the low buildings, and continue peeking out to attack him between his missile salvos or Unibeam attacks.

**8** When his fourth life bar is emptied, Iron Monger goes berserk. He fires a never ending stream of Repulsor attacks, alternating between scatter fire and whitish homing pulsar beams. If you are a long distance from him, use afterburners to fly behind the building closest to Iron Monger. Hover up behind his position, and alter your tactic slightly. To avoid being destroyed while attacking him, activate your energy shields before hover out from the corner to deliver a missile payload and Repulsor fire. As soon as your missiles are away, dodge back behind the building and deactivate energy shields. Reduce the damage sustained during your attacks by advancing only when he is firing reddish scattershot Repulsors. Allow your energy and life support to fully recharge between each strike, and then attack again. Repeat this strategy until Jarvis makes his next announcement.

**9** When Iron Monger's health is but a sliver in his life support bar, Jarvis analyses the situation and determines that he can only be destroyed by grappling him. Hover up to the corner of the building closest his stationary position, then activate your energy shields and fly at him. Quickly grapple him, and tap the Melee/Grapple button rapidly to sever Iron Monger's power cable. This is a crucial and tricky moment, so do not let the opportunity slip!

SYS005    01 3462 21
SYS006    00 1423 11

BIO ACTIVE
VENT ACTIVE

## Destroy the Power Regulators

With Iron Monger defeated, the remaining AIM-X forces take one last stab and defeating Iron Man. Quickly fly to the top of the Stark Industries skyscraper near the center of the stage, and destroy the four power regulators marked in yellow. The aerial forces swarming around the skyscraper's rooftop can be a little overwhelming, so avoid suit failure by leaving your energy shields active the entire time.

When energy or life support wane, drop below the rooftop and hover close to the side of the building. Deactivate energy shields, turn outward and destroy passing fighter jets and gunships. These units are quickly replaced, so do not spend too much time fighting the support units. Return to the rooftop when energy and life support are good, and try to destroy another power regulator before dropping low again.

### THE DAY IS SAVED!

By destroying the power regulators and defeating **Iron Monger**, Iron Man has saved the day. But with plenty of splinter-faction Stark technology buyers still at large in the world, it is doubtful that Tony Stark can retire the Mark III suit just yet. Until the next outing, enjoy the game by trying a more challenging difficulty level, and complete One Man Army missions to unlock more armor suits.

# ONE MAN ARMY

BASICS

ARMOR & UPGRADES

ENEMIES

MISSION

ONE MAN ARMY

SECRETS

One Man Army is a bonus mode where the missions are unlocked by clearing mission in the main game. These missions are played on familiar maps with different rules. The objective in One Man Army mode is to defeat 80 enemies within 10 minutes. Clearing One Man Army missions unlocks additional armor suits for use in Mission Archive and One Man Army modes.

**01 / One Man Army vs. Ten Rings**
Stand as a one man army against the Ten Rings. Defeat 80 enemies within 10 minutes to unlock the Mark II suit.

Ⓐ SELECT   Ⓑ BACK

## ONE MAN ARMY VS. TEN RINGS

This challenge is unlocked by clearing *Mission 03: Stark Weapons*. Eliminating 80 members of the Ten Rings is going to seem like a cakewalk, especially after upgrading some of the Mark III suit's systems to Tech Level 2.

Simply fly from base to base, eliminating all foes. Be sure to grab SAM Batteries wherever available, and use them to destroy other targets.

After the ground forces are greatly diminished, avoid waiting for them to reappear and take to the air. Reroute power to your weapons and shoot down fighter jets until the mission is clear!

## ONE MAN ARMY VS. MAGGIA

Unlock this One Man Army challenge by clearing *Mission 04: Maggia Factories*. Approaching any of the bases causes a large squad of gunships to appear. Therefore, approach each area gingerly, destroying AA Turrets and Missile Turrets while gradually working your way into the center.

When the gunships arrive, try to take the battle to the air just outside the base jurisdiction. Activate Energy Shields if life support runs low.

If you clear out all of the bases and fall just shy of 80 kills, which seems a likely occurrence, then merely take to the skies and shoot down jet fighters until the tally is reached.

# ONE MAN ARMY VS. MERCS

This stage is unlocked by clearing *Mission 07: Arctic Battle*. Approach each base and the village from the lowest altitude, using cliffs to help narrow down enemies as you approach each installation. Trios of gunships hover near each base, and can be easily destroyed by grappling one after another.

Enemies do not reappear on this map, so head over to the airfield when the ground forces are cleared out. Stand near the hangar from which the jet fighters issue, and destroy them as they take off!

# ONE MAN ARMY VS. AIM

Unlock this challenge by clearing *Mission 08: Lost Destroyer*. This mission starts near the lost destroyer, only this time the targets on it are valid enemies. Vehicles and gunships soon roll up on scene, so try not to dive in too quickly. Grappling SAM Batteries and howitzers becomes mission-critical, as it is essential to take down enemies quickly.

After clearing out the destroyer area, proceed toward the bases and fight your way in. Attack the lowest altitude targets first, and work your way upward. Grapple gunships that fly into the scene. Keep a sharp eye on your life support, and activate energy shields and fly away if things turn south.

# ONE MAN ARMY VS. AIM-X

The final One Man Army challenge is unlocked by clearing *Mission 11: Island Meltdown*. Fly in a counterclockwise direction around the islands, destroying one base after another. Start with the lowest altitude targets first, then work your way up. Avoid lingering in any location too long, lest the enemies reappear beneath you.

Grappling SAM Batteries and howitzers and trying to use them against other targets is extremely difficult, so avoid it altogether. When taking on fighter jets flying the skies above, be sure to position Iron Man over the water or a clear area, so that enemies do not reappear below him and attack.

# ACHIEVEMENTS & BONUS MATERIALS

BASICS
ARMOR & UPGRADES
ENEMIES
MISSION
ONE MAN ARMY
SECRETS

## CLEAR GAME BONUSES

Clearing all missions in the Xbox 360 version unlocks the Silver Centurion armor for use in Mission Archive and One Man Army modes. New games can now be played with any unlocked suit.

## XBOX 360 ACHIEVEMENT LIST

| ACHIEVEMENT | G | CRITERIA |
|---|---|---|
| OVERKILL | 15 | DEFEAT A SOLDIER USING THE UNIBEAM |
| IMPENETRABLE | 15 | COMPLETE A MISSION (OTHER THAN ESCAPE OR FIRST FLIGHT) WITHOUT AN ARMOR BREACH |
| GROUNDED | 15 | SUCCESSFULLY GRAPPLE AND THROW A PLANE |
| AN OBJECT IN MOTION | 15 | DESTROY ANY TARGET USING A RAMMING ATTACK |
| YOUR OWN MEDICINE | 15 | DAMAGE OR DESTROY ANOTHER ENEMY WHILE GRAPPLING A SAM LAUNCHER |
| SUICIDAL | 15 | SUCCESSFULLY DESTROY A MISSILE WITH A RAMMING ATTACK |
| LONG SHOT | 15 | SUCCESSFULLY GRAPPLE A HOWITZER |
| HULK SMASH! | 15 | SUCCESSFULLY GRAPPLE AN OPPONENT IN THE HULKBUSTER ARMOR |
| GROUND POUND | 15 | DEFEAT AN OPPONENT USING THE GROUND POUND IN THE EXTREMIS ARMOR |
| PUGILIST | 15 | COMPLETE ANY MISSION (OTHER THAN ESCAPE) WITHOUT USING WEAPONS SYSTEMS |
| AIR SUPERIORITY | 15 | DESTROY ALL DROPSHIPS BEFORE THE STARK GUNSHIP IS STOLEN IN THE FIRST FLIGHT MISSION |
| ROAD KING | 15 | DESTROY ALL CONVOY VEHICLES IN LESS THAN 2 MINUTES IN THE STARK WEAPONS MISSION |
| LAUNCH ABORTED | 15 | DESTROY ALL PROMETHEUS MISSILES WITHIN 10 MINUTES IN THE MAGGIA COMPOUND MISSION |
| COLLATERAL DAMAGE | 15 | DESTROY A PROMETHEUS MISSILE BY DESTROYING A FUEL TRUCK IN THE MAGGIA COMPOUND MISSION |
| PERSONNEL VENDETTA | 15 | DEFEAT 20 SOLDIERS IN THE ARCTIC BATTLE MISSION |
| SMACK DOWN | 15 | DEFEAT TITANIUM MAN BEFORE HIS SECOND RECHARGE IN THE ON DEFENSE MISSION |
| CLASSIC CONFRONTATION | 15 | DEFEAT TITANIUM MAN USING THE CLASSIC ARMOR |
| OLD SCHOOL | 15 | DEFEAT IRON MONGER USING THE SILVER CENTURION ARMOR |
| DISARMED | 25 | DESTROY STOCKPILED STARK WEAPONS IN THE ESCAPE MISSION |
| CITY PROTECTOR | 25 | DESTROY THE DRONES WITHOUT CIVILIAN DAMAGE IN THE FIRST FLIGHT MISSION |
| EJECT! | 25 | SPARE THE US FIGHTER PILOTS IN THE STARK WEAPONS MISSION |
| GUARDIAN | 25 | PROTECT WAREHOUSE WORKERS IN THE MAGGIA FACTORIES MISSION |
| DECOMMISSIONER | 25 | DESTROY ALL PROMETHEUS MISSILES IN THE MAGGIA COMPOUND MISSION |
| IN THE DRINK | 25 | AVOID CIVILIAN CASUALTIES IN THE FLYING FORTRESS MISSION |
| TATYANA, INTERRUPTED | 25 | PROTECT THE NUCLEAR FACILITY IN THE ARCTIC BATTLE MISSION. |
| NOT A SCRATCH | 25 | AVOID HARMING THE DESTROYER AND ITS CREW IN THE LOST DESTROYER MISSION |
| POWER SAVER | 25 | AVOID DISRUPTING THE CITY'S POWER SUPPLY IN THE ON DEFENSE MISSION |
| SHOCKING! | 25 | PROTECT OUTLYING OCCUPIED BUILDINGS IN THE SAVE PEPPER MISSION |
| PROTON SHUT OUT | 25 | PREVENT CANNON ATTACKS ON CIVILIAN TARGETS IN THE ISLAND MELTDOWN MISSION |
| ESCAPE VELOCITY | 25 | SEVER THE TETHER BEFORE THE SATELLITE OVERLOADS IN THE SPACE TETHER MISSION |
| YOU'RE FIRED! | 25 | DESTROY POWER REGULATORS IN THE IRON MONGER MISSION |
| TEN RINGS OBSOLETED | 25 | COMPLETE THE ONE MAN ARMY VS. TEN RINGS CHALLENGE WITHOUT AN ARMOR BREECH |
| MAGGIA OBSOLETED | 25 | COMPLETE THE ONE MAN ARMY VS. MAGGIA CHALLENGE WITHOUT AN ARMOR BREECH |
| MERCS OBSOLETED | 25 | COMPLETE THE ONE MAN ARMY VS. MERCS CHALLENGE WITHOUT AN ARMOR BREECH |
| AIM OBSOLETED | 25 | COMPLETE THE ONE MAN ARMY VS. AIM CHALLENGE WITHOUT AN ARMOR BREECH |
| AIM-X OBSOLETED | 25 | COMPLETE THE ONE MAN ARMY VS. AIM-X CHALLENGE WITHOUT AN ARMOR BREECH |
| EXCELSIOR! | 70 | COMPLETE HERO OBJECTIVES FOR ALL MISSIONS |
| SIDE-KICK | 75 | COMPLETE ALL MISSIONS ON EASY DIFFICULTY (OR HARDER) |
| HERO | 75 | COMPLETE ALL MISSIONS ON NORMAL DIFFICULTY (OR HARDER) |
| SUPER HERO | 75 | COMPLETE ALL MISSIONS ON HARD DIFFICULTY |

# BASICS

## CONTROLS

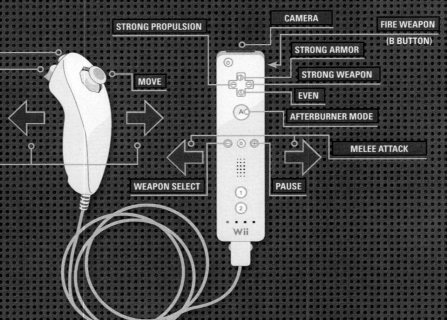

**HOVER**
(HOLD) HOVER UP
(FLICK NUNCHUCK DURING HOVER) DASH

**FREEFALL**

**(FLICK NUNCHUCK) CONTEXTUAL ACTION**

**MOVE**

**STRONG PROPULSION**

**CAMERA**

**FIRE WEAPON**
(B BUTTON)

**STRONG ARMOR**

**STRONG WEAPON**

**EVEN**

**AFTERBURNER MODE**

**MELEE ATTACK**

**WEAPON SELECT**

**PAUSE**

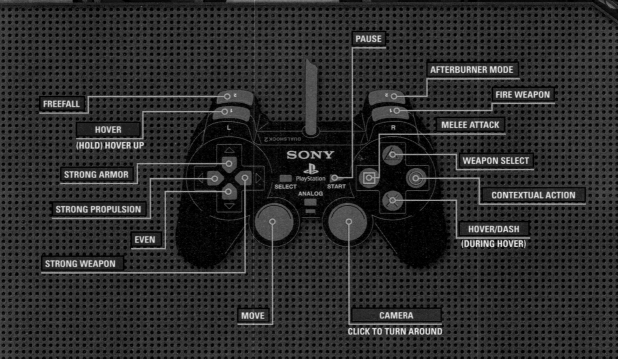

**FREEFALL**

**HOVER**
(HOLD) HOVER UP

**STRONG ARMOR**

**STRONG PROPULSION**

**EVEN**

**STRONG WEAPON**

**MOVE**

**PAUSE**

**AFTERBURNER MODE**

**FIRE WEAPON**

**MELEE ATTACK**

**WEAPON SELECT**

**CONTEXTUAL ACTION**

**HOVER/DASH**
(DURING HOVER)

**CAMERA**
CLICK TO TURN AROUND

# CONTEXTUAL ACTION

Certain tasks throughout the game require you to follow on-screen commands to complete. Things like opening doors and reviving Iron Man's heart require you to press certain buttons or flick the Nunchuck really fast.

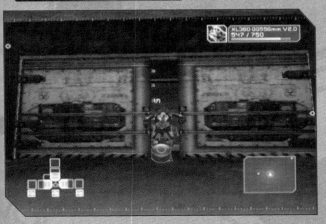

# COMBAT

Most combat is executed from medium- to long-range with Iron Man's Repulsors, Ballistics Weaponry, or Explosives. Use the camera control to place the targeting reticule on an enemy until it turns red. This indicates that the target is locked on. With explosives, you can blind fire near the enemy for a quicker process, but you must still get close so that the splash damage affects the target.

Use the Weapon Select button to cycle through your available weapons: Repulsor, Ballistic, and Explosives. Press the Fire button to shoot at the enemy.

When close to enemies, press the Melee Attack button to hit with Iron Man's armored fists. This becomes an extremely lethal attack once the appropriate upgrade has been obtained.

# CAMERA CONTROL

On the PlayStation 2, the Right Analog Stick controls the camera. The cursor indicates the direction in which Iron Man is facing and you are looking. Move the cursor in the direction you want to look.

With the Wii, the cursor is moved around by pointing the remote at the screen. Move the cursor in the direction you want to look.

SYS001    00 0098 2304112 151
SYS002    00 7802 1023401 674
SYS003    01 6730 2501313 466
SYS004    00 7349 2215919 012

SYS005    01 3462 2109867 990
SYS006    00 1423 1122496 002

BIO ACTIVE
VENT ACTIVE

BASICS
ENEMIES
ARMOR
WEAPONS
UPGRADES
MISSIONS
UNLOCKABLES

You can invert this control so that when you move the camera up you look down and vice versa. Change this in the Control Setting menu.

The cursor changes color when you are targeting an enemy or destructible object. It turns red when an enemy is targeted and yellow when an object can be destroyed.

## HOVERING

Hovering is an absolutely mandatory element to the game and must be mastered before tackling any of the more difficult missions. Tap the Hover button to launch Iron Man into the air and begin hovering. Hold the button to hover higher in the air. When you are ready to come back down, press the Freefall button.

Iron Man always floats in the direction that he's facing (where you are looking) while hovering. Look down to fly descend and up to ascend (unless you have the controls inverted).

Press the Dash button while moving left or right to dodge incoming projectiles and enemy fire. This

uses a bit of energy, but can definitely begin evasive maneuvering. If you have multiple long-ranged missiles or rockets incoming, this is a great tactic to use.

Use your hover to get a good vantage point against groups of enemies. From there you can quickly get away if necessary, dodge their missiles with a Dash move, and rain Explosives and Repulsor shots down on the enemy.

# AFTERBURNER MODE

Use Iron Man's Afterburner Mode to blast from point A to point B. Hold down the Afterburner button to fly through the air. This engages the fastest possible mode of travel and comes into play when time is ticking down on the clock. Whether it's used to prevent a missile launch or save civilians, the Afterburner Mode is something that you'll need to master.

Guide your flight with the Move controls. Combine this with the Camera controls to make a tight turn. For example, while in flight, move to the left and turn the camera to the left to make a tight left turn.

If the Invert Flight option is on, pressing down causes Iron man to fly up and vice versa. Turn this off in the Control Settings, if you like up to be up and down to be down.

Afterburner Mode is also a fantastic way to get far away from trouble and heal up.

# ARMOR

You start the game in the Mark I suit, which uses a Flamethrower as a weapon and has no upgradeability. You then progress to the Mark II suit which focuses on flight and a short weapons tutorial, and by the third mission you use the extremely customizable Mark III suit. Refer to the *Armor* section of this guide for more information on the different suits.

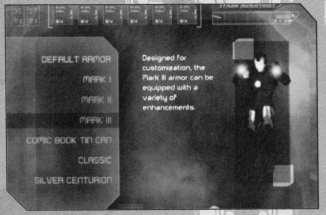

# WEAPONS

In the first mission of the game, you use a Flamethrower. After that you have three different types of weapons: Repulsors, Ballistics, and Explosives. Our *Weapons* section covers these in more detail.

BASICS

ENEMIES

ARMOR

WEAPONS

UPGRADES

MISSIONS

UNLOCKABLES

# UPGRADES

With the Mark III suit, you can upgrade the weapons and the armor itself. Use a weapon on an enemy to earn experience points—the tougher the enemy, the more experience points. A bar under the name of your current weapon in the upper, right corner of the screen shows your progress. When this reaches the end, you have earned the maximum of 100 experience points for that weapon.

You receive the experience toward the type of weapon that was used, or to the suit itself depending on what maneuvers were used during the battle. After a mission, you get statistics on how many experience points toward each weapon you have earned.

Upgrades are automatically unlocked once certain experience levels are reached. You can see what upgrades you have by selecting "Upgrades" from the main menu. Our *Upgrade* section describes the different upgrades and shows when they are unlocked.

# THE SUIT'S SUBSYSTEMS

At any time you can reroute the suit's power to one of the subsystems: Propulsion, Armor, or Weapons. Rerouting power to one of the subsystems not only benefits that subsystem, but can also harm the others. The following sections detail what happens when each subsystem is powered up.

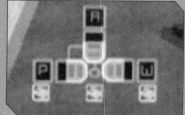

## Strong Propulsion
*(Left on D-pad or +Control Pad)*

This increases your Afterburner Mode speed. Use this when you want to get somewhere even faster than the regular Afterburner Mode. Be sure to change it back once you reach a destination or escape from any enemies that you're fleeing.

Your armor is more vulnerable and weapons are less powerful while the Strong Propulsion is engaged. The Repulsors use energy much faster while in this mode as well.

## Strong Armor
*(Up on D-pad or +Control Pad)*

Strong Armor mode boosts your overall damage resistance. This is enormously effective if you are getting pounded. Switch to this mode when you notice that you're incurring heavy damage, and either hide behind something or flee to a safe spot. Another benefit to this mode is that your melee attacks are more powerful. It's intended for you to be able to trade punches with even the biggest baddies on the block!

However, with Strong Armor activated, the drain on your energy reserves from flying and firing long-range weapons is bigger. You are unable to fly as long and your weapons are weaker. The Repulsors overheat more quickly as well.

## Strong Weapons
*(Right on D-pad or +Control Pad)*

This activates the suit's Unibeam. The Unibeam is more powerful than the regular Repulsors, but

you must charge it up. You are a sitting duck while the Unibeam is charging. Use this against fewer, but tougher enemies—such as a vulnerable boss.

Your armor is weaker in this mode. Therefore, this mode isn't effective against large groups of enemies.

### Even
[Down on D-pad or +Control Pad]

This resets all the subsystems. Don't forget to do this once you're done with a certain mode.

# MANUAL HEART SYSTEM

As you take damage, your armor gets weaker and weaker. This is signified by the Armor meter in the lower left corner of the screen (the vertical bar under the A). If this turns red, fly away to a safe spot, take cover, or hide where you can't be hit.

Iron Man's suit requires quite a bit of power to use and this is delivered through backup power cells. The suit automatically repairs damage. But if it takes too much damage too quickly, you must revive the suit's heart or lose one of the backup power cells.

### Revive Tony's Heart

When your armor is depleted, Tony's heart shuts down from the shock. However, his backup system is phenomenal and allows you a chance to revive his heart with a mini-game. A big picture of Tony's heart is shown surrounded by ten lights. At first,

a single light is lit, indicating that the heart revival system is primed. A line running across the bottom of the screen (that looks very much like an electrocardiogram) indicates how to light up each element.

A specific button is shown below the line. Press the corresponding button when the

line on the graph is just above it. It's based on timing and the correct button choice. Once you're successful with the first input, a set of three more lights activates (2-4).

With three correct button/timing inputs, lights 5-7 and 8-10 light and activate, jumpstarting Tony's heart and giving him another chance at the action. Iron Man is revived!

You can attempt to revive Tony multiple times. However, each successive attempt increases the number of inputs required to activate each set of elements. At first, you only have one input, as described previously. However, a second attempt adds another input to the graph line, requiring two button presses per element. Obviously, a third attempt adds another, and so on. Eventually, you'll fail an attempt and use one of the power cells. This resets the revival mechanic back to a single input per set.

### Backup Power Cells

Underneath the power distribution are three icons. This shows how many backup power cells are

left. You start each mission with three in the Normal difficulty. If you fail to revive the heart, one of these cells is used. If you fail and are out of cells, you fail the mission.

# GAME DIFFICULTY SETTING

When you start a new game, you must choose between Easy, Normal, and Hard difficulties. Easy gives you five backup power cells and enemies cause less damage. Normal gives you three power cells. Hard gives you only one power cell and enemies cause more damage.

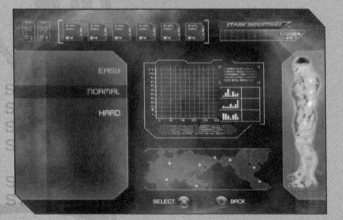

BASICS

ENEMIES

ARMOR

WEAPONS

UPGRADES

MISSIONS

UNLOCKABLES

BIO ACTIVE
VENT ACTIVE

# CHARACTERS

OPTIC ACTIVE

CYB
ROOT
../09:

PAR
ROOT
../03

BOOT JET:23%

77

UNI B

OO

REP BEAM:

67

SPE
TAC...
PLPT.................78%
PLPT.................78%

TEM
OOS...
FAN...
SMO..

LIFE SUPPORT
TYK.................12%

## IRON MAN (TONY STARK)

Billionaire industrialist. Genius inventor. Consummate playboy. While performing a weapons test overseas, Tony Stark was kidnapped and forced to build a devastating weapon. Instead, using his intellect and ingenuity, Tony built a high-tech suit of armor and used it to escape. Upon returning to America, Tony has refined the armor, promising to protect the world as the Invincible Iron Man.

## VIRGINIA "PEPPER" POTTS

Executive assistant to Tony Stark, Pepper has become an indispensable part of Tony's life over the years. Never one to shy away from an argument, Pepper is always there to put out the fires that Tony leaves in his path.

## JARVIS

As the A.I. of Iron Man's suit, this computer-operating system has no personality. Think a next-gen GPS voice that sounds like a British butler.

## LT. COLONEL JAMES "RHODEY" RHODES

Rhodey serves as the military's chief liaison to Stark Industries. Rhodey is also Tony Stark's most trusted ally and best friend.

## YINSEN

Yinsen is a professor who was held in captivity along with Tony Stark. He assists Tony while they're being held prisoner.

# BOSSES

BASICS

ENEMIES

ARMOR

WEAPONS

UPGRADES

MISSIONS

UNLOCKABLES

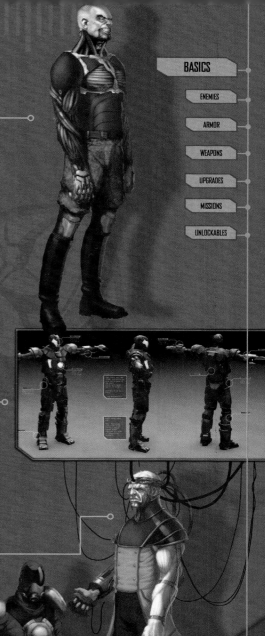

## WHIPLASH (MARK SCARLOTTI)

Mark Scarlotti plays the "tough mercenary" role well, but he's rough around the edges and is ultimately little more than an overpaid thug-for-hire. Currently employed by the Maggia crime family as their No. 1 gun, he was previously employed by Stark Industries.

## WHITNEY FROST

The heir to the Maggia crime empire and an effective, ruthless leader, Whitney Frost is sophisticated, wealthy, and educated. Though she leads the crime syndicate with a good heart, her loyalty to her family often puts her at odds with her own wishes. It's been rumored that she and Tony Stark share a mutual attraction.

## TITANIUM MAN (BORIS BULLSKI)

A relic left over from the Cold War, Bullski is the result of early experiments of genentic manipulation in order to create a breed of "Super Soldiers". He is bent on trying to restore the glory of the Soviet Union and is being tricked by AIM into working for them to help his goals. He's been supplied with a crude version of the Iron Man MK I armor, heavily modified for combat purposes.

## THE CONTROLLER (BASIL SANDHURST)

Basil Sandhurst was a brilliant research scientist involved in "questionable" brain research, which led to an accident that scarred him horribly and caused investors to pull out from funding him. Now he's been contracted by AIM, who will fund his research in exchange for his help.

## THE MELTER (BRUNO HORGAN)

A former employee of Stark Industries, Horgan was driven out of business due to the fact that his product was more primitive and dangerous than Stark's. Now hired by AIM as a weapons research specialist, he's eager to get revenge on Stark.

## IRON MONGER (OBADIAH STANE)

As Tony Stark's right-hand man and a top executive at Stark Industries, Stane is a calculating genius who is willing to do whatever it takes to get the job done. He has been with Stark Industries since before Tony's birth, and was a confidant and advisor to Tony's father, Howard.

00 0090
SYS002    00 7802
SYS003    01 6730
SYS004    00 7349
SYS005    01 3462
SYS006    00 1423 1122496 002

BIO ACTIVE
VENT ACTIVE

PS2 • Wii

# ENEMIES

The following highlights the seven different types of enemies found in your adventures as Iron Man.

## BATTLESUIT

Besides the boss fights, these guys can be your toughest battles. You can pick them off from a distance with a few shots from your Repulsor or some Explosives.

## DRONE

If you aren't taking fire from anywhere else, run up to the Battlesuit and take it down with some melee attacks. Try an EMP blast to disable the Battlesuit before rushing it.

The Drones are mechanized flying turrets that tend not to be much of a threat except in high numbers. Any weapon will take care of these guys.

## HELICOPTER

Keep an eye in the skies for the Helicopters. As you are raining ammunition down on the ground troops, these guys can surprise you from above. Keep an eye on the radar. They can be taken down from afar with the Repulsor.

After taking so much damage, a button icon appears above the Helicopter. Get close enough so that the icon lights up. Press the indicated button and then follow the contextual actions to take it down.

# JEEP

The Jeep is the first vehicle you will come across and it isn't too tough to take down. A few shots from the Repulsor will destroy one.

After so much damage, an icon appears over the Jeep. If you are close enough, the icon lights up. At this point, press the indicated button. Then, follow the contextual actions to flip the Jeep over.

# SOLDIER

Soldiers are the most common enemy in the game. They are only really a threat in big numbers. Use the quick firing Gatling Gun or Pulse Rifle to take them down. Take them down quickly before concentrating your effort on the tougher enemies.

Watch out for the Soldiers with rocket launchers. Try to take out these guys first. They will do much more damage than the Soldiers with Ballistic guns.

BASICS

ENEMIES

ARMOR

WEAPONS

UPGRADES

MISSIONS

UNLOCKABLES

# TANK

Out of all of the enemies, Tanks have the best defense. It takes several shots from the Repulsor or Explosives to take one down. After getting the ElectroPunch upgrade, you can use your melee attack to defeat a Tank.

Use an EMP attack to disable the Tank and then press the indicated button to jump onto the Tank. Follow the contextual actions and Iron Man will rip the gun off the Tank and smash it into pieces.

# TURRET

There are several varieties of Turrets that shoot all types of ammunition. These guys are easy to target since they don't move. You can take them down from a distance with the Repulsor or Explosives. These are often the first line of defense. In some locations you can sweep the perimeter taking these guys out first.

# ARMOR

You play through each mission with a default suit of armor. For the first mission you use the Mark I suit. The second mission puts Tony in his new creation, Mark II. After that, you use the advanced and upgradeable Mark III suit.

After completing certain missions, you can play back through in the following suits. This only changes the way Iron Man looks, they still function like the default armor. Refer to the Unlockables section for information on when the suits are unlocked.

Tony Stark crafted the first-ever Iron Man Suit as the prisoner of militants in Afghanistan. With the help of Yinsen, he constructed this key instrument to his heroic escape.

**MARK I**

Tony constructed the Mark II with an emphasis on exploring flight potential. As the first suit of Iron Man armor built at Stark Industries, the Mark II armor was soon replaced by the Mark III.

**MARK II**

Designed for customization, the Mark III armor can be equipped with a variety of enhancements.

**MARK III**

BASICS

ENEMIES

ARMOR

WEAPONS

UPGRADES

MISSIONS

UNLOCKABLES

This first ever Iron Man suit was built during the character's initial appearance in *Tales of Suspense* #39, and this design originates from the interpretation from *Iron Man* Vol. 4 #5.

**COMIC BOOK TIN CAN**

Iron Man's first iconic armor was finalized in *Tales of Suspense* #66. It was the first suit to feature the trademark palm-mounted Repulsors.

**CLASSIC**

Sporting new colors, Tony used this suit during his fight with Iron Monger, his days as a West Coast Avenger, and in the first "Armor Wars" storyline.

**SILVER CENTURION**

# WEAPONS

For the first mission, Escape, Tony's Mark I armor uses only the Flamethrower weapon. Mark II uses the Repulsor. Mark III gives you access to three different types of weapons: Repulsors, Ballistics, and Explosives. Use one of these types of weapon to earn experience and gain upgrades that improve your weapons.

## EXPLOSIVES

Explosives are the most powerful of your weapons, but are really limited in supply. They are also slower to fire than your other weapons. Save these for the tougher enemies, like Tanks.

### ROCKETS

These explosives pack a nice punch, but are a little slow. You need to aim ahead of moving targets to hit them. The final upgrade for the Rockets adds an EMP charge that disables any mechanical enemies in the area.

### MISSILES

You get the Missile Launcher after upgrading the Rockets to a certain point. Upgrade to the Auto Targeting System to make aiming easier. You can also hold down the Fire button to launch more missiles. Move the reticule over multiple enemies to hit more than one enemy at a time.

## FLAMETHROWER

The Flamethrower is extremely powerful with limited range. It is only available in *Mission 1: Escape* on the Mark I suit.

## UNIBEAM

The Unibeam is upgraded after the Repulsor has been upgraded. Redirect the suit's power to the weapons to enable the Unibeam. The chest beam is a powerful weapon against vehicles. You must fully charge the weapon to fire it, which is its one downfall. Iron Man is a sitting duck while charging; be careful when trying to use this weapon in the face of a horde of enemies.

## REPULSOR

Repulsors are Iron Man's main weapon. It will take care of anything you come across. The problem with it is that it drains energy pretty quickly, especially if you have re-routed power elsewhere. The Repulsors are great from long-range and even more so once you get the Longer Range upgrade.

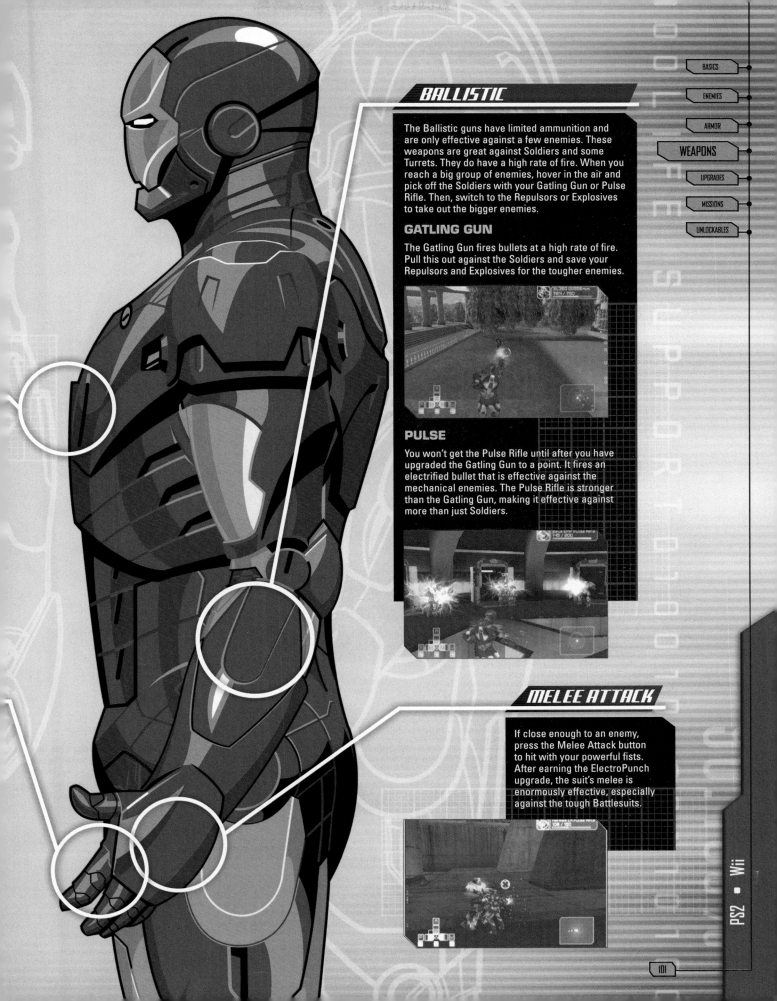

BASICS

ENEMIES

ARMOR

WEAPONS

UPGRADES

MISSIONS

UNLOCKABLES

## BALLISTIC

The Ballistic guns have limited ammunition and are only effective against a few enemies. These weapons are great against Soldiers and some Turrets. They do have a high rate of fire. When you reach a big group of enemies, hover in the air and pick off the Soldiers with your Gatling Gun or Pulse Rifle. Then, switch to the Repulsors or Explosives to take out the bigger enemies.

### GATLING GUN

The Gatling Gun fires bullets at a high rate of fire. Pull this out against the Soldiers and save your Repulsors and Explosives for the tougher enemies.

### PULSE

You won't get the Pulse Rifle until after you have upgraded the Gatling Gun to a point. It fires an electrified bullet that is effective against the mechanical enemies. The Pulse Rifle is stronger than the Gatling Gun, making it effective against more than just Soldiers.

## MELEE ATTACK

If close enough to an enemy, press the Melee Attack button to hit with your powerful fists. After earning the ElectroPunch upgrade, the suit's melee is enormously effective, especially against the tough Battlesuits.

## UPGRADES

### Floor Punch

By cutting Iron Man's thrusters when high enough, the Iron Man suit will drop to the ground, creating a small shockwave capable of incapacitating nearby enemies.

### Power Stomp

This system disables the auto-hovering system when above a vehicular enemy, allowing the Iron Man suit to be used as a crude spear, inflicting great damage to anyone who happens to be under it at the time.

DAMAGE AMMO RANGE SPEED

DAMAGE AMMO RANGE SPEED

ACTIVATE LIFE SUPPORT

BASICS
ENEMIES
ARMOR
WEAPONS
UPGRADES
MISSIONS
UNLOCKABLES

## Electro Punch

Creates electro-magnetic fields around Iron Man's fists, thereby increasing the amount of damage done by hand-to-hand attacks. This gives your melee attacks much more power, making it a great alternative when low on ammo and your Repulsor is out of energy.

## Turbo Boost

Get this upgrade to increase movement speed, both in hover mode and in flight mode. This is helpful when dodging an enemy's explosives or when trying to get away.

## NanoTech Knitters

This increases the regeneration rate of the Armor sub-system. Take cover when Iron Man is nearing heart failure and your armor heals faster after getting this upgrade.

## Kamikaze

When in Strong Propulsion Mode, Iron Man can punch through all enemies destroying them instantly. Warning: Iron Man's armor will take a certain amount of damage, depending on the type of enemy. Reroute Iron Man's power to Propulsion and go into Afterburner Mode. Fly right through enemies to take them out without using any ammo.

## Repulsor Floor Punch

This upgrade creates a larger shockwave when Iron man drops from a greater altitude. After laying down some fire in a group of enemies, drop from high above to save on ammo and take out multiple enemies at a time.

## Anti-Missile System

Automatically destroys missiles that are in close range to Iron Man, at a rate of 1 per second. This system consumes some energy when in use.

# BALLISTICS
## UPGRADES

- DAMAGE
- AMMO
- RANGE
- SPEED

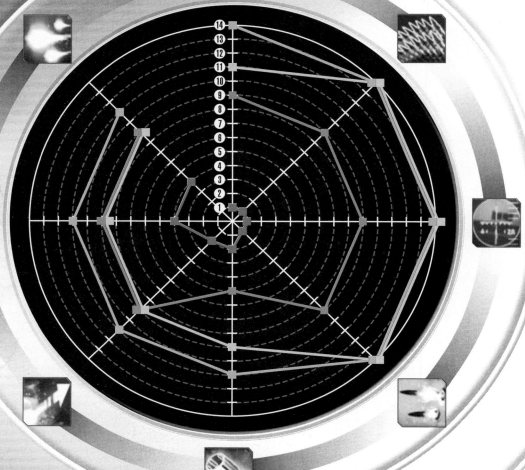

### Light Gatling Gun

Standard-issue minigun. High fire rate and low accuracy. Perfect against troops, but inefficient against heavy vehicles.

DAMAGE
AMMO
RANGE
SPEED

### XL360 GG556mm

A minigun with a larger magazine, able to hold more bullets.

DAMAGE
AMMO
RANGE
SPEED

DODIIIOIOI IOIOIOIII O OI OO ACTIVATE LIFE SUPPORT ODIO IOIOI

BASICS

ENEMIES

ARMOR

WEAPONS

UPGRADES

MISSIONS

UNLOCKABLES

## XL360 GG556mm V2.0

Using an advanced ballistic sub-system, this minigun has much greater accuracy than the previous models.

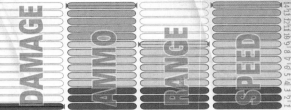

## Hermes LR Pulse Rifle

An upgraded ballistic computer array along with a new barrel shape allows for much greater range for this pulse rifle.

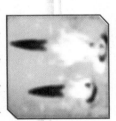

## XL360 GG556mm V3.0

A special blend of titanium and adamantium makes the bullets used by this minigun even more damaging.

## Hades LC Pulse Rifle

A larger magazine makes this already great weapon even better.

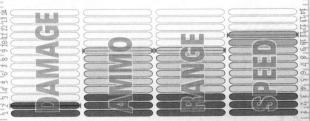

## Ares Pulse Rifle

Gun that fires an electrified bullet, which is capable of dealing more damage than a regular minigun.

## Zeus EMP Pulse Rifle

Improving on the electrical charge allows for this weapon's bullets to deliver a non-fatal EMP blast, disabling mechanical enemies for a short period.

# EXPLOSIVES

## UPGRADES

- DAMAGE
- AMMO
- RANGE
- SPEED

### Excelsior Rockets

The best micro-rockets money can buy.

DAMAGE AMMO RANGE SPEED

### Excelsior 2.0 Rockets

These smaller rockets still pack the same punch as their larger cousins, but with the added advantage of allowing the Iron Man suit to carry more for the same weight.

DAMAGE AMMO RANGE SPEED

0000110101 10101111 0 01 00 ACTIVATE LIFE SUPPORT 0010 10101

BASICS

ENEMIES

ARMOR

WEAPONS

UPGRADES

MISSIONS

UNLOCKABLES

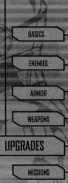

## Meteor MH Rockets

Rockets with an added twist; the warhead separates on impact, discharging an additional 3 micro-rockets, for that extra BOOM.

DAMAGE · AMMO · RANGE · SPEED

## Bloodhound 2.0 Missiles

A better magazine design allows a larger amount of guided missiles to be launched simultaneously. Hold down the Fire button and move the reticule across multiple enemies to hit more than one at a time.

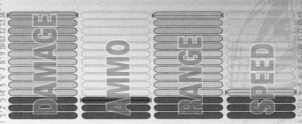

DAMAGE · AMMO · RANGE · SPEED

## Thunderbolt EMP Rockets

An EMP charge in the warhead allows for a large EMP blast centered around the point of impact, temporarily disabling any mechanical enemies in the area. Note that only the initial target gets hard damage, all other targets are simply disabled temporarily.

DAMAGE · AMMO · RANGE · SPEED

## Sunspear Missiles

An auto-targeting system allows the Iron Man suit to automatically target enemies in its front arc, allowing its user to concentrate on navigation.

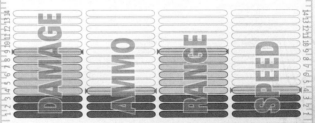

DAMAGE · AMMO · RANGE · SPEED

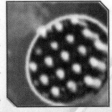

## Bloodhound Missiles

Fire-and-forget missiles, mainly for use against vehicles.

DAMAGE · AMMO · RANGE · SPEED

## Sunspear 2.0 AGMS

A better propulsion system and a more aerodynamic fin sub-assembly make this missile more nimble than its predecessors.

DAMAGE · AMMO · RANGE · SPEED

# REPULSOR
## UPGRADES

- DAMAGE
- AMMO
- RANGE
- SPEED

Level up weapons by using them and unlock more powerful versions. Taking out enemies earns experience points toward the weapon that was used. The tougher the enemy the more experience points you get. Try to split your time with the three weapons during each mission to maximize your experience.

After a mission, the game shows you how much experience out of 100 you received for each weapon. For each 100 points toward a weapon, the next upgrade for that weapon is unlocked. For each 100 points toward the Suit, the next Armor upgrade becomes available.

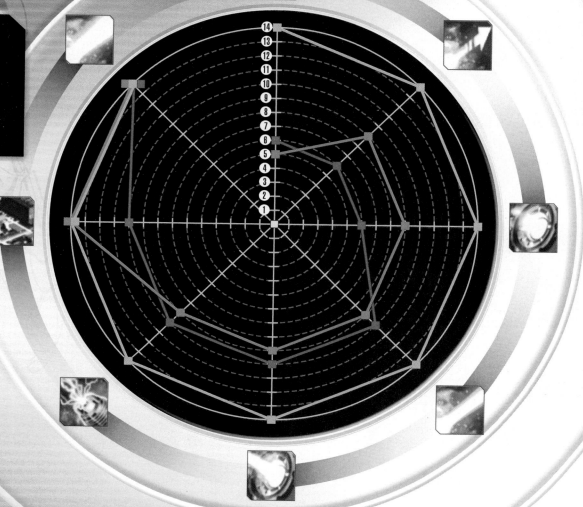

### Repulsor Technology

Repulsors use the latest technology developed by Tony Stark right before he was kidnapped. They are capable of dealing non-lethal damage at a great range and come in two basic flavors: quick-firing hand-based version and powerful, but slow-charging chest-based Unibeam.

DAMAGE
AMMO
RANGE
SPEED

### Repulsor Longer Range

Changing the base polarity of the Repulsors and Unibeam just before it exits the firing chamber helps reduce the air friction on it, therefore allowing them to reach much further than before.

DAMAGE
AMMO
RANGE
SPEED

BASICS
ENEMIES
ARMOR
WEAPONS
UPGRADES
MISSIONS
UNLOCKABLES

## Improved Build-Up

A new switch design coupled with a better capacitor sub-assembly allow for a much faster charge up time in this version of the Unibeam.

DAMAGE   AMMO   RANGE   SPEED

## Energy Generator

A complete overhaul of the basic mechanics of the Heart sub-system allows for greater generation of energy when in the field.

DAMAGE   AMMO   RANGE   SPEED

## Improved Damage Level

Using a double capacitor coupling along with a better alloy for wiring has allowed the Repulsors and Unibeam to now deliver a much greater concussive charge.

DAMAGE   AMMO   RANGE   SPEED

## Improved Thermal Switch

Advances to the energy management system allow for greater switching speed when energy is re-directed.

DAMAGE   AMMO   RANGE   SPEED

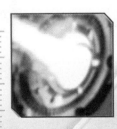

## Unibeam Extra Range

By bypassing the thermal regulator and feeding the energy directly into the Unibeam, a greater range is achieved with this version of the weapon.

DAMAGE   AMMO   RANGE   SPEED

## Optimal Beam Damage

A new design for the base capacitor gives this version of the Repulsors and Unibeam a much greater punch.

DAMAGE   AMMO   RANGE   SPEED

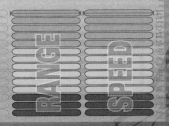

PS2 • Wii

# 1 ESCAPE

## MISSION DESCRIPTION

*Cobbled together from available parts, the means of your escape are finally complete. Defeat your captors and clear a safe path out of the area.*

## MISSION OBJECTIVE

ESCAPE FROM CAPTIVITY.

## COLLATERAL OBJECTIVES

FLEE FROM YOUR PRISON CELL.

MAKE YOUR WAY THROUGH THE CAVERNS.

DESTROY THE LAST OF THE WEAPON CRATES.

## DEFAULT ARMOR

MARK I          MARK II          MARK III

## WEAPONS & AMMO

 WEAPON CRATES

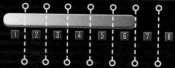

AMMO BOXES

## ENEMIES

SOLDIERS

TURRETS

## Flee from your Prison Cell

Once Tony Stark completes his suit of armor, Yinsen helps him get acquainted with it. This first level serves as a tutorial for using the Mark I armor. Move out of the first room to receive your first objective: Flee from your prison cell.

### NEVER LOST

**A blue dot marks Iron Man's next waypoint and indicates the distance from his current position. Use this point to find the next objective. Once you reach a waypoint, another often appears in the distance until you reach the final destination.**

Move toward the door ahead to acquire the Melee Attack. Use it to destroy the door.

BASICS

ENEMIES

ARMOR

WEAPONS

UPGRADES

MISSIONS

UNLOCKABLES

## Make your Way through the Caverns

Next you receive the Flamethrower attack. Toast the Soldiers as you progress through the cave. The path splits a couple of times, so look everywhere to clear them all out.

### EXPLOSIVES

**Explosive barrels are all around the level. Use them to take out any Soldiers unlucky (or dumb) enough to be next to these barrels of destruction.**

At the top of the slope, use the Flamethrower on the wooden boards to knock them down. Take out the Turret ahead and don't miss the Soldier to the right of the rock wall. Continue to follow the waypoints and continue on.

## Destroy all the Stark Industries Weapon Crates

 A Soldier is firing on your position from a ledge to the right. Look up and fry him. Continue on to find the first Weapon Crate; destroy it! Lay waste to more Soldiers as you proceed, but watch out for the RPG Soldier on the ledge to the left.

### OBJECTS DESTROYED

**There are boxes and debris littered about the level. If the reticule turns yellow when aiming at an object, it can be destroyed.**

At the ledge ahead, Tony Stark learns the real power of his suit by dropping down on a couple of unsuspecting enemies. Free-falling from a good height and landing on the ground causes a Shockwave that takes out nearby Soldiers.

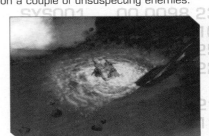

SYS005    01 3462 2109867 990
SYS006    00 1423 1122496 002

BIO  ACTIVE
VENT  ACTIVE
RESP  FLTR  ACTIVE
OPTIC  ACTIVE

|||||||||    ||||||| ||| ||||||||

CYBERNET  ...
ROOT: 3845788959 OSU
../09: 290582394 -303

PART GEN  ...-4283-003 FRT
ROOT: 3842533379 OSU
../03: 290783394 -303

BOOT JET:23%...

771 DLP

UNI BEAM:49%...

003 OMP

REP BEAM: ||||  ||  |||| ||| | | |||

675 %

SPEED
TNC...........
PLPT...........
PLPT...........

TEMP
ODS...........
FAN...................88%
SMO...................28%

LIFE SUPPORT
TYK...................12%

Move up the ramp to hear from Yinsen again. Continue forward, taking out any Soldiers you come across and destroy the second Weapon Crate. It is too late to save Yinsen, but you can head up the narrow path on the right to get revenge on the Soldier above. Continue following the waypoints ahead across the wooden bridge, using your melee attack and Flamethrower to clear the way. Destroy the third Weapon Crate as you run up the slope.

## Dodge the Rockets

Once outside, take immediate notice of the Soldier ahead with an RPG. Take cover behind the rocks and make your way toward the Soldier, moving from rock to rock. Don't forget to torch all the other Soldiers along the way. Remain behind the rocks as much as possible to avoid the rockets.

Once you're close enough, aim at the Soldier above and take him out with your Flamethrower. Running to the left to take out more Soldiers and destroy the fourth Weapon Crate is also an option. Next, dash up the ramp to the ledge where the RPG Soldier once stood.

Traverse the bridge to find another Turret and Soldier and drop off the right side of the bridge to take out more Soldiers with your Shockwave. The fourth Weapon Crate is just waiting for you to destroy it.

## Back into the Cave

Run back into the cave and destroy anyone and anything in your way. Take the left path as it splits. This leads to the fifth Weapon Crate. Both paths farther ahead take you out of the cave, but take the right path to reach an upper ledge.

## Destroy the Last of the Weapon Crates

Decimate the Soldiers here before dropping down to the ground. There are a couple Turrets on the right and Soldiers guard the sixth Weapon Crate. Destroy everything here before following the waypoint to a gate. Unleash your attack on the gate until it opens and enter the enemies' secret stash. Destroy the last Weapon Crates to finish the first mission.

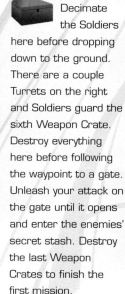

BASICS

ENEMIES

ARMOR

WEAPONS

UPGRADES

MISSIONS

UNLOCKABLES

# 2 FIRST FLIGHT

## MISSION DESCRIPTION

*With the full resources and technology of Stark Industries at your disposal, you have honed the concepts behind the original Iron Man armor into a technological marvel. Test the Mark II armor's capabilities in the skies above Stark Industries.*

## MISSION OBJECTIVE

TEST THE NEW IRON MAN SUIT.

## COLLATERAL OBJECTIVES

HOVER THROUGH THE BEACONS.

FREE-FALL TO PERFORM A FLOOR PUNCH.

FLY THROUGH BEACONS USING AFTERBURNER MODE.

COMPLETE THE WEAPON TRAINING.

ENGAGE THE MERCENARIES.

DEFUSE C4 CHARGES.

DEFEAT THE STOLEN HELICOPTER.

## DEFAULT ARMOR

MARK I          MARK II          MARK III

## WEAPONS & AMMO

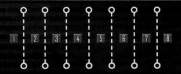

WEAPON CRATES

AMMO BOXES

1  2  3  4  5  6  7  8

## ENEMIES

HELICOPTER          SOLDIERS

4X4S

### Hover through the Beacons

As this mission begins, Iron Man's Heart Monitoring System becomes operational. A meter in the top-left corner shows his health and Jarvis is now online and to help test the Mark II suit.

The first objective is to learn how to hover with this new suit, so begin by hovering through the beacon above, and then continue by dropping back down through another beacon.

## LEARN TO HOVER

**Refer to the *Basics* section for more information on how to control Iron Man in the air for the different consoles.**

## CONTROL YOUR HOVER

**Iron Man always hovers in the direction you are looking while hovering. Look down to hover downward and up to fly upward.**

SYS001          00 0098 230

SYS002          00 7802 102

SYS003          01 6730 250

SYS004          00 7349 221

SYS005          01 3462 210

SYS006          00 1423 11

BIO  ACTIVE

VENT ACTIVE

PS2  ▪  Wii

SYS005    01 3462 2109867 990
SYS006    00 1423 1122496 002

BIO  ACTIVE
VENT  ACTIVE
RESP  FLTR  ACTIVE
OPTIC  ACTIVE

|||||||    |||||||

CYBERNET   2-4987-000-AR
ROOT: 3845782372 OSU
.../09: 29058299 909

PART GEN
ROOT: 384253
.../03: 290785

BOOT JET:23%

771 DLE

UNI BEAM:49%

003 OM

REP BEAM: |||| |||

675 %

SPEED
TNC..............
PLPT..............
PLPT..............

TEMP
ODS..............
FAN..............
SMO..............

LIFE SUPPORT
TYK..............12%

More beacons appear in the air. Fly through each beacon in succession. Look for the blue beacon and fly through it, at which point the next beacon turns blue. The next beacon also appears on your radar if you lose track of it. Use a dash to reach the next beacon more quickly.

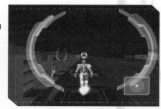

After you hover through all of the beacons, a final beacon appears on the ground ahead. Land inside this beacon to complete the objective.

### Drop to the Ground to Perform Floor Punch

Hover high in the air and head to the beacon in the distance. After flying through it, drop to the ground to cause a devastating shockwave. Iron Man's Floor Punch is a weapon that shouldn't be overlooked, so remember it when faced with heavy infantry forces!

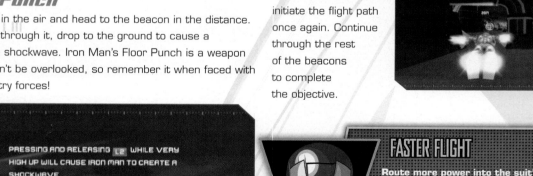

PRESSING AND RELEASING L2 WHILE VERY HIGH UP WILL CAUSE IRON MAN TO CREATE A SHOCKWAVE.

### Fly through Beacons Using Afterburner Mode

Iron Man must fly through the next beacons in Afterburner Mode to complete the objective. Hold down the Afterburner button and head for the beacon ahead.

## AFTERBURNER MODE

Find more information on how to fly in Afterburner Mode in the *Basics* section of this guide.

Keep the pointer in the middle of the next beacon to line yourself up. It is tough to get started, but once in flight, things become smoother. Things get tight at times. If you hit something, you have to re-engage Afterburner Mode and initiate the flight path once again. Continue through the rest of the beacons to complete the objective.

### FASTER FLIGHT

Route more power into the suit's Propulsion for more speed in flight. Be careful though; granting the suit's thrusters this much power can cause it to be more difficult to control.

BASICS

ENEMIES

ARMOR

WEAPONS

UPGRADES

MISSIONS

UNLOCKABLES

## Complete the Weapon Training

Fly to the next waypoint to begin your weapon training. Repulsors become available as targets appear both ahead and behind Iron Man. Take out each with a shot from the Repulsors. The next phase of the test requires that you shoot down a couple moving targets. Destroy them with the Repulsors to quickly end this segment of the mission.

## Unibeam Mark I

Now you get to try out Iron Man's Unibeam. Re-route power to Weapons to activate it and hold down the Fire Button to charge the beam fully. Release the button after charging the weapon to fire a full blast at each target to complete weapon training.

Head to the next waypoint and follow the on screen commands to open the hanger door. Here you find Maggia's Soldiers attacking Stark Industries.

## Engage the Mercenaries

Use the Repulsors to take down the Soldiers outside. Fly to the next waypoint and eliminate a few additional Soldiers and two 4x4s. It's possible to use Iron Man's Unibeam to take out the 4x4s in a single shot, but he's a sitting duck while charging it It's best to remove as much of the surrounding infantry as possible before attempting this.

Once the 4x4s are gone, re-route power to Iron Man's armor for more resistance from the Soldiers' firepower. Hover around the area and decimate any remaining Soldiers.

## Defuse C4 Charges

Iron Man is informed that C4 has been placed on a nearby train. Spin around to find the waypoint that marks the C4 location and engage the Afterburners to reach it in no time. Follow the on-screen command once you reach the C4 to defuse it.

## Defeat the Stolen Helicopter

Watch out! An enemy pilot has stolen a Stark Industries Helicopter and you must take it down to prevent the technology from falling into their hands. Relentlessly fire Iron Man's Repulsors at the Helicopter until it is destroyed. Well done!

SYS001          230
SYS002          102
SYS003          250
SYS004    00 7349 22

SYS005    01 3462 21
SYS006    00 1423 11

BIO ACTIVE
VENT ACTIVE

PS2 • Wii

# 3 FIGHT BACK

## MISSION DESCRIPTION

*Your former captors have hidden several caches of Stark weapons throughout the area. Find them and cripple their military capacity.*

## MISSION OBJECTIVE

DESTROY THE WEAPON CACHES.

## COLLATERAL OBJECTIVES

DESTROY THE WEAPONS CACHES WITHOUT HARMING ANY CIVILIANS.

HACK COMPUTER TO GAIN INFORMATION.

DESTROY THE DREADNOUGHT.

## DEFAULT ARMOR

MARK I          MARK II          MARK III

## WEAPONS & AMMO

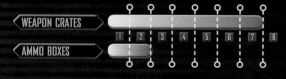

WEAPON CRATES   1 2 3 4 5 6 7 8

AMMO BOXES

## ENEMIES

4X4S            TURRET

SOLDIERS        DREADNOUGHT

## *Destroy the Weapons Caches without Harming any Civilians*

Jarvis has located three weapon caches and it is up to Iron Man to destroy them. You gain control of Iron Man hovering above a small town infested with enemy Soldiers. During the intro to this mission, you may have noticed another group of houses on the left side of the ravine as you flew by. Head back to that point and find the first Weapon Crate lying in front of the houses. Start picking off the Soldiers and 4x4s below, but stay alert! Watch out for the missiles from the RPGs; shoot them down or dodge to the side and evade them.

Complete a circular circuit around the town, destroying the entire enemy force as you go. Your first priority is to remove the missile launching enemies. Watch where the missiles come from and target the Soldiers firing them. A Weapon Crate is on the far side of town—directly opposite from where you began this mission. Finish the initial mission at the waypoint on the other side of town. Enter the hole on the side of the building.

## Free the Civilians

Drop to the floor below and use Iron Man's destructive melee attack against the cage's bars to free a Civilian. There's also

a Weapon Cache
inside the room!
The enemy knows
that Iron Man can't
indiscriminately fire on
the Weapon Crates
with civilians around!
Eliminate the Weapon
Crate to remove the
potential threat of
having it in enemy
hands. The resulting
explosion reveals a
passage to a hidden
tunnel!

## Refill your Weapon Supply at the Ammo Box

 Enter the
tunnel and
follow the bridges to the
ledge above. Continue
out the other side to
find an Ammo Box.
This refills Iron Man's
ammunition supply.

A few Soldiers and a 4x4 are just outside; take care of them to attract more enemies intent on keeping Iron Man from wiping out their hidden caches. Hover high into the air to find a bridge spanning the area between two ledges. Use the Repulsors or the Gatling Gun on the Soldiers to each side. Wipe them out!

## Keep an Eye Out for Weapon Crates

 Enter the cave on the right and continue until
you reach the farthest wall inside. Drop to the

ground below and
turn 180 degrees
to find another Stark
Industries Weapon
Crate. Destroy it and
leave the cave. Head
up the hill and continue
through the tunnel.

Stop before the buildings ahead and hover into the air. Launch some Rockets at the 4x4s to destroy them. There are Soldiers throughout this open area. Keep moving to avoid their fire and take them out with Iron Man's Repulsors or Gatling Gun.

 Once they are removed from the battle,
drop to the ground and look for another
Weapon Crate to destroy. It's at the base of the houses
on the far side from where you entered. Once that crate

is destroyed, scan
to the left from your
current position to find
yet another Weapon
Crate. It looks like
they're running out of
hiding spots and are
resorting to piling the
crates together!

BASICS
ENEMIES
ARMOR
WEAPONS
UPGRADES
MISSIONS
UNLOCKABLES

Look for the next waypoint and head out. Enter the nearby garage and eliminate the Soldiers inside. Refill your ammunition supplies at the Ammo Box in the back. Get ready for some more action!

## Free More Civilians

Drop into the hole in the floor to discover another Civilian being held in a cell. Crush the bars to free more of the captured Civilians. Once again, the enemies have hidden a Weapon Cache inside the cell with innocents. Obliterate it to reveal an entrance into another cave. The tunnel leads to another cell! Free these Civilians and destroy the final Weapon Cache. Doing so exposes the entrance to another cave.

## Hack the Computer to Gain Information

Follow the cave past the point at which it splits to find another hidden Weapon Crate. Return to the split and head up the other path. Look out! There are more Soldiers and they seem intent on protecting their final Weapon Crate!

Continue through the cave until you find the exit. Remain just inside the doorway and eliminate the 4x4s outside with Iron Man's Repulsors. Continue into the new area and continue to decimate any Soldiers inside the structure from a safe distance. Once the threat has been reduced, proceed inside and eliminate the rest.

Follow the corridor through a door, but stop before entering the second door. Once again, utilize the cover of the doorway to take out as many Soldiers as possible from this safe position before continuing inside.

Move to the left side of the room first to discover the final Weapon Crate hidden amongst the rest of the boxes. Watch out for the Soldiers on the walkway above; blast them from below, or hover up to them to crush them face-to-face.

Completely clear out the big room and exit through the other door to find the computer.

Hack into it to complete this secondary objective. The big door opens at the far end of the big room to reveal a Maggia Dreadnought! They're not playing around any more!

BASICS

ENEMIES

ARMOR

WEAPONS

UPGRADES

MISSIONS

UNLOCKABLES

# MAGGIA DREADNOUGHT

**1** The Dreadnought is armed with two rocket launchers, one on each side, and a pulse gun in its center. Each weapon has its own health bar and must therefore be taken out individually. A monster like the Dreadnought isn't going to fall when one of its weapons is obliterated! It's going to fight to the bitter end!

**2** The Dreadnought occasionally releases a spherical EMP attack that knocks Iron Man back if he gets too close. If you see this attack coming, use the Afterburner to get away to a safer distance.

**3** Concentrate all attacks on a single weapon at a time. The fight becomes a bit easier as the threats are picked off one at a time, so continue utilizing this focused attack tactic until they are all eliminated. Once the three ranged weapons are removed, the only attack you must worry about is the one with limited range. Move to the other side of the area and launch a barrage of Rockets at the Dreadnought. Aim at a point just ahead of it as it moves from side to side. The perfect time to fire a Rocket is when the Dreadnought begins charging up its EMP attack.

**4** After several direct Rocket hits, the Dreadnought explodes in a burst of metal and flames. This ends the threat of the Maggia Dreadnought and the mission.

## MISSION DESCRIPTION

*Rhodes has informed you of a large stockpile of weapons hidden in the area. Follow an enemy transport vehicle to find them.*

## MISSION OBJECTIVE

DISRUPT MAGGIA'S OPERATION IN THE REGION.

## COLLATERAL OBJECTIVES

REACH THE VILLAGE WHERE THE CONVOY IS LOCATED.

FOLLOW THE CONVOY WITHOUT DESTROYING IT.

DEFEAT MARC SCARLOTTI.

## DEFAULT ARMOR

MARK I            MARK II            MARK III

## WEAPONS & AMMO

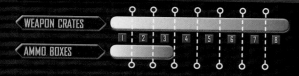

WEAPON CRATES    1 2 3 4 5 6 7 8

AMMO BOXES

## ENEMIES

HELICOPTERS

4X4S

SOLDIERS

TANKS

MARC "WHIPLASH" SCARLOTTI

### Reach the Village Where the Convoy is Located

Fly towards the waypoint ahead to locate the transport. Along the way, take out the Soldiers atop the two towers and on the ground. Take time to blast the first Weapon Crate at the base of the left tower.

### Follow the Convoy without Destroying It

The convoy is just ahead to the left. Take out as many Soldiers around the truck from a distance before moving in to obliterate the second Weapon Crate, which is behind the truck.

The truck starts up and begins driving once you reach the waypoint. Stay close behind the truck and *do not* fire at it! Take out the Soldiers and 4x4s on each side of the road as you follow the truck. The truck reaches its first stop after a short trip down the road. Get ready for some action!

## PLAY CATCH-UP

If you fall behind, use the Dash move or Iron Man's Afterburners to catch back up. You can be in front of the truck as long as you don't get too far ahead. If you hear Jarvis say, "The Truck is getting away," stop immediately and wait for the truck to reach you or return to the truck.

BASICS

ENEMIES

ARMOR

WEAPONS

UPGRADES

MISSIONS

UNLOCKABLES

## First Stop

Fire a few Rockets on the Tank that shows up to shoot Iron Man out of the air and take out the Helicopter above with the Repulsors. Refill your ammunition at the box just ahead of the truck's location. There are two Weapon Crates, one before the stopped truck and another after, that are just waiting for you to scrap them. Don't miss that chance!

### RIP THE TOPS OFF THE TANKS

After a Tank takes enough damage, an icon appears above it. Hover just above the Tank and press the indicated button to attempt to rip the turret off. Follow the on-screen commands to completely destroy the Tank. Be careful though, this takes a while to complete and you run the risk of losing the truck if it's on the move.

When the truck begins moving once again, get behind it and continue to follow. Watch out for the enemies that litter the sides of the road—including a couple Tanks and a Helicopter. Crush the opposition as you pace the truck.

## Second Stop

The transport reaches another stop where a couple Tanks are waiting for Iron Man. Launch Rockets their way to obliterate them both and continue clearing out any remaining enemies. There's an Ammo Box and a Weapon Crate in a location just before the second stop. You will also find a Weapon Crate inside the garage. After a short while, the transport starts back up again.

Two Soldiers are just down the road and they're firing RPGs from a bridge and they're being covered by two Tanks below the bridge. That's quite a formidable force! Launch Rockets as soon as the Tanks come within view! Removing them from the battle allows you to target the Soldiers with the Repulsors or Gatling Gun.

Watch out for a Tank and Soldier hiding along the truck's path, just ahead to the right. Hover until you see the Tank behind the trees, then take it out with some Rockets. The Soldier shouldn't pose too much of a threat after the Tank's gone.

## Third Stop

After a couple of right turns, the transport reaches another stop. Locate the Ammo Box on the left side of the road at the second right turn. Obliterate the Weapon Crate that's just to the right of the truck's parked location.

## Final Stop

The Truck starts back up for its final trip. A couple 4x4s, Soldiers, and Helicopters guard the road. Take them out with Iron Man's Repulsors. Two Tanks are waiting for Iron Man at the Transport's final stop, but they blow up just as easily as any other when introduced to a few Rockets.

Take out the Tanks with Rockets and use the Gatling Gun on the surrounding Soldiers. Remain in the air and assume a continually maneuvering posture to evade incoming missiles.

There is an opening just beyond the stopped truck that leads back to a fortress wall. Find the final Weapon Crate on the wall.

BASICS
ENEMIES
ARMOR
WEAPONS
UPGRADES
MISSIONS
UNLOCKABLES

# WHIPLASH

**1** Drop through the opening and run down the corridor to find the stockpile of weapons. Mark Scarlotti is in the next room and drops in on you. Watch out! There is no time for pleasantries since he immediately launches an all-out attack!

**2** Scarlotti has his shield up most of the time. Iron Man's attacks are useless while Whiplash's shield remains up. Avoid him and his attacks as he runs around—just stay on the move. When Scarlotti stops, he unleashes his whips to attack Iron Man. However, to do so, he must drop his shield and reveals his vulnerability. Avoid his attack and launch a couple attacks during the short time his shield is down. If you are close enough, crush him with a melee attack; otherwise, just fire the Repulsors at him.

**3** After a few hits, Scarlotti vanishes. After a short while, you notice a blue blob on the ground that indicates where Scarlotti is going to land. Watch out! If you do not avoid this, Scarlotti attacks from above and inflicts some solid damage. Avoid this attack a few times until Scarlotti returns to his original attack process. Once again, focus your attacks during the small window of opportunity provided while his shield is down.

**4** Continue scoring a couple attacks each time he lets his guard down and keep evading his attacks the rest of the time. Eventually, you deplete Scarlotti's health and watch as he falls. Great job Iron Man! Mission complete.

## MISSION DESCRIPTION

*Maggia's production facilities have been destroyed leaving most of their remaining weapons at their fortress-like headquarters with military-grade defenses. Maggia saw fit to attack Stark Industries—it's time to return the favor.*

## MISSION OBJECTIVE

FIND OUT WHAT MAGGIA IS UP TO.

## COLLATERAL OBJECTIVES

DESTROY THE CONTROL BUNKERS.

PREVENT MISSILES FROM BEING LAUNCHED.

DESTROY THE BLAST DOOR SHIELDING THE MAIN DOOR.

REACH THE LOWEST LEVEL OF THE FACILITY.

REACH FROST'S COMMAND CENTER.

DEFEAT FROST.

## DEFAULT ARMOR

MARK I          MARK II          MARK III

## WEAPONS & AMMO

WEAPON CRATES    1  2  3  4  5  6  7  8

AMMO BOXES

## ENEMIES

| | |
|---|---|
| HELICOPTERS | TURRETS |
| SOLDIERS | FROST |
| TANKS | |

## Destroy the Control Bunkers

Iron Man begins the mission in front of the Maggia Compound. Jarvis has marked the locations of the bunkers with waypoints. Iron Man needs to find the bunkers and destroy them to eliminate the ground-to-air threat they present.

Start off by using Iron Man's Repulsors on the Soldiers immediately ahead and take out the Turret at the front right corner of the compound. Approach the building and take out the Turret above each of the front two bunkers.

## Prevent Missiles from Being Launched

Start attacking one of the two bunkers. Soon after you initiate your attack, a Prometheus Missile is detected and it seems that it's being primed for launch. You must reach it at the opposite side of the compound and destroy it before it can launch. This isn't some small warhead here, it's a fully armed Prometheus Missile that can potentially threaten a large number of people! Get on it!

BASICS

ENEMIES

ARMOR

WEAPONS

UPGRADES

MISSIONS

UNLOCKABLES

## COMPLETELY DESTROY THE BUNKERS

Be sure to completely destroy the bunkers before moving on. A fully obliterated bunker is indicated by:
1) the disappearance of the waypoint and 2) smoke billowing from the crushed bunker.

## The Third Control Bunker

Eliminate the Soldiers and Turrets atop this building and then face to the left to find another bunker. Take out the Turret on top, but don't miss the Weapon Crate atop the previous building. Take the time to destroy the crate before completing the destruction of the third bunker.

Take out the Turret atop the nearby bunker and put some Rockets into the two Tanks below. Look around this area and destroy everyone and everything you see. There are no friendly targets nearby—only enemies.

Fire a few shots from the Repulsors at the third bunker—another missile appears ready to launch. The Maggia simply aren't fooling around! This Prometheus Missile silo is in a fountain in the middle of the compound—right in plain sight! Dash over to the missile location and wipe out everything in the area, focusing on the missile itself.

## The Second Control Bunker

A Weapon Crate is right next to this building and an Ammo Box is right by the helipad. Eliminate as many of the enemies around the area before refilling your ammunition.

Destroying the bunker in this location primes yet another missile which is prepping for launch. Spin the camera around until you locate the waypoint and fly that way to find the missile.
Don't waste any time! Get over there and take the missile out with all the means at your disposal!

## The Fourth Control Bunker

The fourth bunker is straight ahead on top of the mansion. Take out the Turret and any other enemies hanging around. Destroying this Bunker triggers the appearance of two Tanks, one on each side of the compound. Obliterate them with some Rocket blasts.

PS2 ■ Wii

125

## The Fifth and Sixth Control Bunkers

Annihilate the two bunkers on each side of the complex near the smoking hulks of metal that were once the Tanks that you just eliminated. Be sure to completely destroy the Bunkers before moving on! If they retain even one bar of health, they'll remain to fire on Iron Man! A Weapon Crate can be found on the ground next to a wall near one of these bunkers.

Watch out for any Helicopters that appear in the sky above. Don't hesitate to blast them out of the air with a few shots from Iron Man's Repulsors.

## The Seventh Control Bunker

There is a single bunker left at one of the front corners of the complex—it's directly opposite the first bunker you destroyed. More Tanks and Helicopters appear along with some Soldiers to aid in its defense. Take care of them all.

## The Final Control Bunker

There should now be one waypoint left marking the final Control Bunker. Fly over to it, destroy the Turret, and eradicate any remaining enemies in the area. Use Iron Man's melee strikes on the bunker until you see the tell-tale sign of destruction—smoke.

After destroying the final bunker, the Maggia's final Prometheus Missile is prepped for launch at the far corner of the complex. Use Iron Man's Afterburner Mode to reach it in time and obliterate their final weapon of mass destruction.

Fire Rockets at the Tanks that appear in vain to defend their territory. Blow the Helicopters that show up out of the skies with Iron Man's Repulsors. Once the skies are clear of enemies, and only husks of enemy vehicles are smoking on land, it's time to enter the mansion.

## Destroy the Blast Door Shielding the Main Door

Go to the front door and destroy the blast door with several melee attacks. Enter the mansion.

BASICS

ENEMIES

ARMOR

WEAPONS

UPGRADES

MISSIONS

UNLOCKABLES

## Reach the Lowest Level of the Facility

Next you must find the control room. Jarvis suggests that it is in the lower level, 200 feet down. Move across the room and take out the Soldiers that suddenly appear. It looks as if the remaining soldiers have pulled back to defend the manor house.

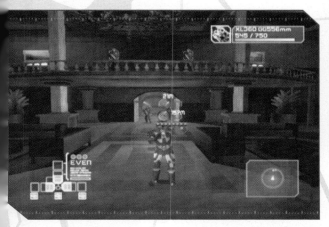

Run down the hallway to find a Medusa-like sculpture firing some type of beam down the hall. There are a series of sculptures down each side with space between them.

Wait for the ray to stop and dodge forward to one of these "safe" spaces. Continue advancing this way until you reach the end of the hall. Turn to the right and take out the Turret on the ceiling and the Soldiers nearby.

### DESTROY THE SCULPTURES

You can either avoid the rays or destroy the Medusa-like sculptures with a few shots from Iron Man's Repulsors.

Another Medusa-like sculpture periodically fires a beam down the next hall. Again, use the spaces along the two sides to dodge its attack and take out the Soldiers found hiding along the way.

Turn left at the end of this hall to flush out a few more Soldiers. Take them out and proceed to the waypoint. Press the indicated button to blast a hole in the floor. Drop through to reach the lower level.

## Reach Frost's Command Center

Step into the big room ahead and blast anything and anyone you see. Be careful of the two Turrets hanging from the ceiling. Take them out with a couple shots from the Repulsors.

Advance to the back of the room being careful not to step on the blue mines on the ground. Hover over them to the big door and press the indicated button. Follow the on-screen commands to open the door.

PS2 ■ Wii

## DETONATE THE MINES

Once located, the mines can be detonated from a distance. Fire some shots at the mines to blow them up from safety.

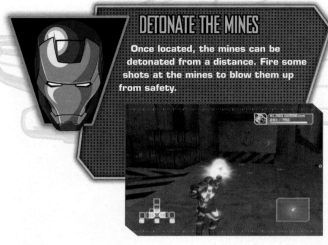

Watch out! There are more mines lying in front of the next door. Hover over them or detonate them from a distance and open the door.

There's another door at the back of the room; follow the commands presented to open it. Head down the next hall, taking out the Turrets and Soldiers that get in your way. Refill your ammunition at the Ammo Box in the short hallway on the left.

Follow the hallway into another room where a Weapon Crate is hidden behind some gray boxes. Continue around the corner to find another big room.

Take out as many Soldiers as possible before entering the room. Launch some Rockets at the Tank on the left to decimate it, but watch out. Another Turret is firing from the ceiling above. Yet another Weapon Crate is hidden behind some additional gray boxes in the far corner.

# WHITNEY FROST

**1** In the next room, three bull heads are mounted on the far wall. Much like the Medusa-like sculptures before, these bulls periodically blast straight beams down the areas directly in front of them. This means that there are three potential areas where Iron Man can take serious damage from the bull heads. Hide behind the columns to avoid the attacks.

**2** Focus on the bull heads on the side first! Use Iron Man's Repulsors to quickly fire a couple shots at the bull heads before retreating behind the safety of the columns. Don't get too comfortable behind the columns though, wall panels may open up on the flanking sides of the room revealing Soldiers intent on reducing Iron Man to scrap! Take out the Soldiers while the wall panels are open before resuming your attack on the bull heads.

**3** Repeat this process until the first bull head has been destroyed. The Soldiers become more of an annoyance after phase 2 is reached and you may find that one Soldier may occasionally emerge through the hole created by the destruction of the bull head. Keep an eye out for them as you repeat this whole strategy on the bull head mounted on the other side.

**4** Once the two side heads are gone, focus your attacks entirely on the center head. The center head shouldn't take too long to finish off, and after several blasts from Iron Man's Repulsors, a hole is blown into the wall revealing another room.

**5** Enter the room and use the computer to finish the mission. Once again, Iron Man has proven himself nigh invincible!

**1**

**2**

**3**

**4**

**5**

304111
02340
250131
221591
62 210986
123 112245

BIO
VEN
RES
OPTIC  ACTIVE

CYBERNET   2-4987-000-AF
ROOT: 3845782372 OSU
.../09: 290582394 -303

PART GEN   7-4333-003-FF
ROOT: 3842532372 OSU
.../03: 290783394 -303

PS2 ● Wii

BOOT JET:23%

**771** DLP

## MISSION DESCRIPTION

*You've identified Maggia's last remaining stronghold, a flying fortress that serves as an airborne military staging area. Destroy it and end Maggia's reign of villainy for good.*

## MISSION OBJECTIVE

DESTROY THE FLYING FORTRESS.

## COLLATERAL OBJECTIVES

FIND A WAY TO DISABLE THE MAIN CANNONS.

REACH CENTRAL DATA STORAGE.

DISABLE SURGE PROTECTION CIRCUITS ON THE FOUR REACTORS.

OPEN THE LOADING BAY DOORS.

GAIN ACCESS TO MAIN ENGINE CONSOLE AND CREATE POWER SURGE.

DESTROY MINES BEFORE THEY REACH CIVILIAN TARGETS.

## DEFAULT ARMOR

MARK I          MARK II          MARK III

## WEAPONS & AMMO

## ENEMIES

HELICOPTER          SOLDIERS

DRONES          TURRETS

## Find a Way to Disable the Main Cannons

Jarvis has detected a radar jamming device located on the bottom of the ship. Fly under it and take out the six Turrets hanging from the underside. The radar jamming device is on the other side. Destroy it to regain Iron Man's radar.

Watch out for the rockets being fired by Soldiers standing along the middle body of the fortress. Destroy them and obliterate the four Turrets mounted on the top.

Next to the radar jamming device is an octagonal shaped hatch. Shoot it out and hover into this secret area for a Weapon Crate and Ammo Box.

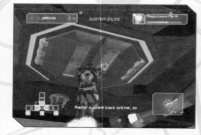

Helicopters appear after two cannons are disabled. Use the Repulsors to take them down, then launch some Rockets at the final two cannons to complete the objective.

## Reach Central Data Storage

 A door opens on the fortress and a squad of Soldiers pours out. Arm Iron Man's Gatling Gun and take them out while advancing to enter the ship. Follow the hall down until you reach a door on the left. Bust it open to discover both an Ammo Box and a Weapon Crate.

Take out the Soldiers in the next room and access the computer. Watch out for the mines on the floor. Shoot them out or hover over them. More Turrets activate outside and the fortress begins firing missiles.

## Disable Surge Protection Circuits on the 4 Reactors

Return outside to locate the four circuits that must be disabled; one is located at each corner near the engines. Eliminate the Drones and Helicopters with Iron Man's Repulsors and dodge the incoming missiles as you head to one of the corners.

## AVOID THE MAIN CANNON FIRE

Avoid the fire from the Cannons as you eliminate the Turrets and Soldiers. You know a cannon is preparing to fire when the shield protecting it disappears for a second, provided you haven't taken down the generators. If you see this, dash to the side and evade the incoming barrage.

There are four main cannons on the top of the ship and they are shielded unless you've taken out the generators.

Concentrate on one cannon at a time. Time the shots for awhile and anticipate when they're going to fire. Start firing Iron Man's Repulsors just as the shield drops to get a shot in during the short time that it becomes vulnerable.

After one of the cannons has been disabled, Drones show up to fight you off. Blow them out of the sky as they appear before returning your attention to the cannons. Time the shield drops and obliterate the next cannon.

Fly up to a circuit and press the indicated button. Follow the on-screen commands to disable the circuit. Quickly fly down the side of the fortress and take out the second circuit. Watch out for the Drones along the way!

Fly under the ship to the other side to find the last two circuits, continually avoiding the missiles along the way. Disable them in the same way as the other two.

## Open the Loading Bay Doors

Fly to the front of the ship to the door marked on the radar. Follow the on-screen commands to open the door and find more Soldiers inside. Use the computer inside to open the loading bay doors.

## Gain Access to Main Engine Console and Create Power Surge

Reload your weapons with the Ammo Box before heading back outside. Take down any Helicopters that arrive while avoiding the missile barrage that continues to engulf you.

## Destroy Mines before They Reach Civilian Targets

Next, mines are launched from the bottom of the fortress one at a time. Quickly fly underneath the flying behemoth and take down each mine before it gets away. A short cinematic indicates when a new mine is launched.

### TAKE OUT THE MISSILE LAUNCHERS

The missile launcher located below the EMP gun, as well as the missile launcher outside, can be destroyed with the Repulsor or Explosives. You can also hit them with some melee attacks to the side.

In between mines, enter the loading bay at the front of the fortress and fire the Gatling Gun at the Soldiers within. Don't miss the Stark Industries Weapon Crate in the back.

Launch a well-placed Rocket at the EMP gun above to gain access to the main engine console. After destroying another mine, enter this opening and follow the path to another computer. Correctly press the indicated button to have Iron Man initiate a power surge that destroys the flying fortress and completes the mission.

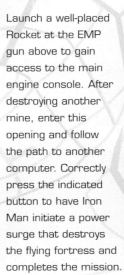

BASICS

ENEMIES

ARMOR

WEAPONS

UPGRADES

MISSIONS

UNLOCKABLES

# NUCLEAR WINTER

## MISSION DESCRIPTION

*Advanced Idea Mechanics (AIM) has been linked to the takeover of a remote Arctic nuclear facility. Investigate why Stark Industries top buyer is involved in militarily seizing a Russian power plant.*

## MISSION OBJECTIVE

STOP THE THEFT OF RADIOACTIVE MATERIAL.

## COLLATERAL OBJECTIVES

SECURE ALPHA AND BETA NUCLEAR WASTE DEPOTS.

SEAL THE OPEN CASKETS IN BETA DEPOT.

CLOSE THE DEPOT DOOR BETA.

SEAL THE OPEN CASKETS IN ALPHA DEPOT.

CLOSE THE DEPOT DOOR ALPHA.

DESTROY THE CARGO TRAIN.

SECURE THE LAST WASTE DEPOT.

DEFEAT TITANIUM MAN.

## DEFAULT ARMOR

MARK I    MARK II    MARK III

## WEAPONS & AMMO

| WEAPON CRATES | | | | | | | |
|---|---|---|---|---|---|---|---|
| 1 | 2 | 3 | 4 | 5 | 6 | 7 | 8 |

| AMMO BOXES | | | | | | | |
|---|---|---|---|---|---|---|---|

## ENEMIES

| | |
|---|---|
| HELICOPTER | TANKS |
| 4X4S | TURRETS |
| SOLDIERS | TITANIUM MAN |

## Secure Beta Nuclear Waste Depot

You begin the level hovering in front of two waste depots. Both must be secured. Start off with the closest building on the left, the Beta Depot. Fly over to the entrance and take out the 4x4s, Tanks, and Helicopter that arrive.

### FIRST WEAPON CRATE

**Before flying over to the Beta Depot, look in front of the first building on the right past the cooling towers.**

Enter the building and use your Ballistic weapon on the Soldiers inside. Follow the halls down through a few rooms, taking out any Soldiers along the way. Refill your weapons at the Ammo Box and keep an eye out for the Weapon Crate in the next room. Destroy it and move on.

## Seal the Open Caskets in Beta Depot

Continue down the hall until you reach a room with several caskets inside. Four are open and must be sealed. Close the two on the upper floor by pressing the indicated button as it appears.

Look down to the lower floor and take out the Soldiers patrolling below. Hop down and close the other two caskets when the enemies have been eliminated.

## Close the Depot Door Beta

There is still a radiation leak, so you must close the door to ensure the safety of everyone else present. Run up to the entrance of the room and follow the on-screen commands to close the door.

Hover back up to the entrance of the building taking out the Soldiers that have arrived to reinforce the enemies that patrolled the halls. Once you reach the building entrance, follow the commands to close the door and secure the Beta Depot for good.

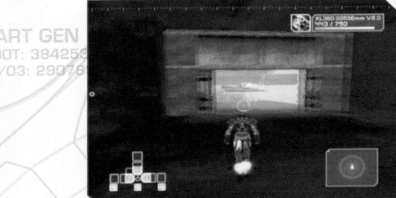

## Secure Alpha Nuclear Waste Depot

Fly over to the Alpha Depot and proceed inside. Just as you did in the Beta Depot, use your Ballistic weapon on the Soldiers as you advance through the halls. It's best not to leave any roaming behind you. Don't miss the Weapon Crate in the back corner.

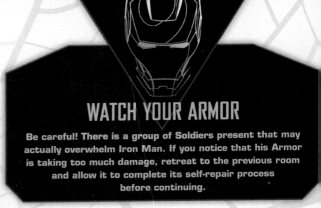

## WATCH YOUR ARMOR

Be careful! There is a group of Soldiers present that may actually overwhelm Iron Man. If you notice that his Armor is taking too much damage, retreat to the previous room and allow it to complete its self-repair process before continuing.

BASICS

ENEMIES

ARMOR

WEAPONS

UPGRADES

MISSIONS

UNLOCKABLES

## Seal the Open Caskets in Alpha Depot

When you reach the final room, you find two more open caskets that need sealed. Take out the Soldiers from just outside the room and then proceed to close the caskets.

## Close the Depot Door Alpha

Follow the on-screen commands to close the door to this room to prevent any residual radiation from leaking out to threaten anyone else. Hover back through the halls, eliminating any Soldiers that are foolish enough to get in your way. At the building entrance, follow the commands to close the doors for good.

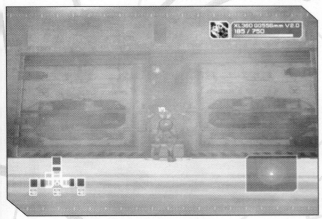

## Destroy the Cargo Train

Once you return outside after sealing both Alpha and Beta Depots, you notice that a train has been loaded and is preparing to leave. You must destroy it before it gets away.

Fly down the length of the train and take out the Turrets mounted on top with Iron Man's Repulsors. Immediately switch to your Rockets and take out the Tanks guarding the train. Leave only scrap!

Launch some Rockets at each section of the train until it has been destroyed. More enemies arrive as you continue to battle the train. Either continue to dodge the incoming fire or take them out as they appear to reduce the threat level.

## Secure the Last Waste Depot

A final depot must be secured before this mission can be considered a success. Take out the enemies patrolling the grounds outside with a combination of Repulsors and Ballistics.

## EXTRA AMMO

There's an Ammo Box just outside the depot in the open area near the train. Reload Iron Man's ammunition when the weapons are running low.

Run down the ramp to find the entrance to the depot. Pick off the Soldiers guarding either side of the first room and follow the hall down to a large, open room.

 Continue down the path until you reach a big, open room. Carefully hover around the outside of the room and pick off the Soldiers with Iron Man's Repulsors. There's a Weapon Crate lying on the middle platform behind some boxes.

Advance down the ramp to find more Soldiers holed up to the right. Continue around the corner, picking off the Soldiers as soon as they're spotted.

# TITANIUM MAN

**1** A hallway is the exit out from this room, but it leads directly into danger! Out of the frying pan, into the path of a green blast of destruction! It leads directly to Titanium Man!

## AVOID THE CONTAINMENT UNITS

The most important element to watch out for during this battle is to avoid hitting the containment units surrounding the stage. If one takes too much damage it explodes and expels a blast of radiation that would threaten the entire region. Destroy too many containment units and the mission will be considered a failure!

**2** When Titanium Man moves to one of the Containment Units and attempts to absorb some radiation, quickly fly up to him and knock him off with a couple of melee attacks. If you can't reach him in time, fire a few shots at him. However, keep in mind that long-range fire destroys the containment unit in addition to preventing Titanium Man from powering up. As long as you keep the destruction to a minimum and refrain from destroying too many of them, the battle will continue.

**3** When Titanium Man attacks with his pulse gun, stay on the move and fly in an evasive pattern to avoid taking damage. Eventually, he'll stop his barrage and hunch over—he's vulnerable now! Hit him with a couple shots from Iron Man's Repulsors while he's catching his breath.

**4** Be ready for him to cross his arms over his chest! This indicates that he's charging a point-blank, area of effect radiation blast and explodes. This inflicts considerable damage to Iron Man if he is too close. Take your cue and dash as far away as possible when you see him begin this attack. Time the blast to the best of your ability! Once he completes the attack, he again loses his shield and becomes vulnerable to Iron Man's counterattack. Fire a couple shots from the Repulsors to return the favor and bring him down a notch.

**5** Continue avoiding his attacks and retaliating while he's vulnerable when his shield is down. Eventually Titanium Man will fall against the might of the Invincible Iron Man! Mission complete.

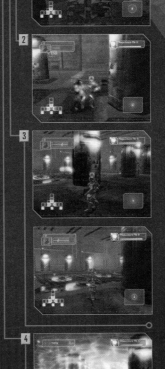

30411
02340
50131
21591

10986
12249

7-000-AR
SU
303

PART GEN   7-4333-003-FR
ROOT: 3842532372 OSU
.../03: 290783394 -303

BOOT JET: 23% |||| || | |||||

771 DLP

UNLBEAM: 49% |||| | | || ||

## MISSION DESCRIPTION

*The military has lost communication with a prototype aircraft carrier. All signs suggest the involvement of AIM, and with it, the use of Stark Industries weaponry. Recover the ship, save the crew, and eliminate any AIM threats.*

## MISSION OBJECTIVE

FIND OUT WHO IS BEHIND THE THEFT OF THE PROTOTYPE AIRCRAFT CARRIER.

## COLLATERAL OBJECTIVES

BREAK THE FIRST LINE OF DEFENSE.

OPEN THE HATCH OF THE CARGO BAY.

RESCUE THE COMMAND CREW.

DESTROY THE CRATES CONTAINING THE REACTOR PARTS.

PREVENT THE RUSSIAN FROM LEAVING WITH THE SECOND REACTOR.

## DEFAULT ARMOR

MARK I        MARK II        MARK III

## WEAPONS & AMMO

| | 1 | 2 | 3 | 4 | 5 | 6 | 7 | 8 |
|---|---|---|---|---|---|---|---|---|
| WEAPON CRATES | | | | | | | | |
| AMMO BOXES | | | | | | | | |

## ENEMIES

DRONES                TANKS

HELICOPTER            TURRETS

SOLDIERS             CONTROLLER

### Break the First Line of Defense

There are 11 enemies that you must eliminate before getting inside. Make your way down the ship picking off the Soldiers, Tanks, and Turrets along the way.

Shortly after engaging in battle, you receive an incoming message from the Controller saying that he has taken control of the electrical activity of your mind! You start to see double and must use the control stick to line up the two images. If you fail, your movement control is reversed: Up is Down, Left is Right...

Once you eliminate seven of the requisite 11 enemies, a couple Helicopters show up to harass you further. The Controller once again attempts to take over your mind, forcing you to align the images to retain proper control. Take down the rest of the enemies as quickly as possible.

## USE THE RADAR

**Refer to your radar to locate the rest of the enemies. Look for their red dots on the screen and head their way.**

BASICS

ENEMIES

ARMOR

WEAPONS

UPGRADES

MISSIONS

UNLOCKABLES

## Open the Hatch of the Cargo Bay

With the required number of enemies downed, Jarvis marks the location of the switch to the cargo bay hatch as more Soldiers and Drones arrive to prevent Iron Man from infiltrating their latest find. Enter the room and use the switch on the left. There's an Ammo Box just inside the room. Reload Iron Man's weapons if necessary and get ready to rescue the crew.

## Rescue the Command Crew

Drop into the newly opened cargo bay and shoot down the Drones buzzing around. After eliminating the last Drone, the shield drops and frees the command crew. Well done Iron Man!

## Destroy the Crates Containing Reactor Parts

The locations of the crates containing parts for the first reactor have been marked on Iron Man's radar. Leave the cargo bay and destroy the Helicopter and Soldiers waiting to blast Iron Man out of the sky!

Fly to the side of the ship to locate an opening that will allow you inside. Take out the Soldiers just within the entrance and continue in to find the Controller.

Once again, he uses his considerable abilities to attempt to control Tony's mind! Match up the two images to avoid having your movement controls reversed.

Use the Right Analog Stick

Switch to Rockets and launch a few at the Tank barring your way. Then, obliterate the Soldiers surrounding the husk that was the Tank. Four Drones join the fight, but you're not about to be stopped now!

 Once you have eliminated the enemy threat, destroy the five crates indicated on the radar. The Ammo Box sits next to the final crate. Two Helicopters arrive to reinforce the decimated enemy forces, but succeed in creating a new hole in the side of the ship.

## Prevent the Russian from Leaving with the Second Reactor

Take down the two Helicopters and fly up the coast following the waypoint. Use Rockets to take out the Tanks and the Repulsors to blast the Helicopters out of the skies. The convoy eventually comes within range, so unleash some of that Repulsor firepower to destroy the trucks and complete the mission.

# 9 HOME FRONT

## MISSION DESCRIPTION

*You return to Stark Industries searching for answers. Why is AIM willing to go to such great lengths to acquire power sources? What are they trying to develop?*

## MISSION OBJECTIVE

SURVIVE TITANIUM MAN'S ASSAULT.

## DEFAULT ARMOR

MARK I          MARK II          MARK III

## WEAPONS & AMMO

WEAPON CRATES

AMMO BOXES

| 1 | 2 | 3 | 4 | 5 | 6 | 7 | 8 |

## ENEMIES

HELICOPTER          TANKS

SOLDIERS          TITANIUM MAN

## *Survive Titanium Man's Assault*

Iron Man arrives back at his company only to discover that his empire is being attacked by AIM! This time they are after Iron Man, and Titanium Man has taken the lead. There's no point in letting them wait too long...

Step into the opening, pull out Iron Man's Ballistics weapon or Repulsors, and start picking off the Soldiers encroaching on Stark property. Keep moving as you circle the area, taking out any enemies you find.

After taking down a few of the Soldiers, Titanium Man arrives for revenge after taking a beating earlier. However, it seems as if he hasn't learned too much during the time off he had after his last defeat. He did bring more friends this time though. The method to Titanium Man's defeat is the same as it was at the end of the Nuclear Winter mission. Only this time, AIM Soldiers surround you and continue to attack while you're engaged with their boss; this makes your job much more difficult.

### REFILL AMMO WHEN NEEDED

Two of the back, right buildings from where you start this mission are open. Find an Ammo Box in the back building. Save it for when you run low on ammo.

BASICS

ENEMIES

ARMOR

WEAPONS

UPGRADES

MISSIONS

UNLOCKABLES

With so many enemies surrounding you, it is easy to become overwhelmed. Take out the Soldiers first and as quickly and efficiently as possible. Once their numbers are significantly reduced, concentrate your fire on any Helicopters and/or Tanks that are advancing.

Continue moving around and eliminate the reinforcements that continue to arrive. If you maintain a solid counterattack tactic, avoiding incoming fire and hitting Titanium Man when his shield is down, Iron Man should have no problem defeating him once again.

## STAY ON THE MOVE

As you are fighting, stay on the move and don't hover in a static position for too long. Avoid the rockets and pulse beams fired your way and retain an evasive strategy.

With the Soldiers out of the way for now, focus entirely on Titanium Man. Wait for him to finish his attack and drop his shield. At this time, fire a few shots from the Repulsors to drain his health a bit.

## KEEP AN EYE OUT

Retain a good amount of distance between you and Titanium Man in case he unleashes his radiation explosion attack. As you circle the area, try to keep him in view as much as possible. Use the radar as well, since you can get a good idea of his position without continually keeping him in sight.

## MISSION DESCRIPTION

AIM has kidnapped Pepper and is holding her hostage at a research facility. You recognize the obvious trap, but only one option exists: Save Pepper

## MISSION OBJECTIVE

SAVE PEPPER

## COLLATERAL OBJECTIVES

FIND THE AREA WHERE PEPPER IS BEING HELD.

OPEN THE TAINTER GATE.

DISABLE THE EMP EMITTERS.

PREVENT AIM FROM DESTROYING THE MAIN LAB.

PREVENT THE MISSILES FROM DESTROYING THE MAIN COMPLEX.

DESTROY THE CONTROL CENTER.

## DEFAULT ARMOR

MARK I          MARK II          MARK III

## WEAPONS & AMMO

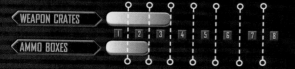

WEAPON CRATES
AMMO BOXES

## ENEMIES

BATTLESUITS          TANKS

HELICOPTER          TURRETS

SOLDIERS

### Find the Area where Pepper is Being Held

You start the mission in a ravine just down the way from a dam. Fly along the water until you find the dam itself. There's a gate at the bottom of the dam, and Jarvis has marked the location of the switch for you.

### Open the Tainter Gate

Fly toward the window until you notice the Turrets—one on each side of the window. Take them out with a couple shots from your Repulsors. Blow out the window and take out the two Soldiers running toward the switch. Land inside and use the switch to open the gate.

### Introducing Battlesuits

Enter the now-open gate and take out the Soldiers waiting inside. There are a couple Battlesuits holding the position along with the Soldiers. These guys require a bit more firepower to eliminate. Share a bit with them. Once the mobile enemies are down, notice that there is a pair of Turrets on each side of this big room. Blow them away with Iron Man's Repulsors before destroying the Weapon Crate located on the ground on the left side.

Follow the hallway ahead and hover up the shaft to find a lone Turret mounted on the ceiling. Crush it with a couple Repulsor blasts.

Continue down the long hall and look into the room on the left. A pair of Battlesuits guards the room from any armored presence that's not their own—this means Iron Man. Take them out with Repulsors or Missiles. Dodge back out to the hall when you have to allow the suit's armor to build back up. Fly up the shaft and quickly take down the three Soldiers above. Use

the computer to close a gate in the previous hall, and open a new one. Drop back down the shaft and turn left; follow the newly opened hall.

## Disable the EMP Emitters

This drops you into the area where Pepper is being held. Unfortunately, three EMP transmitters in the area are disrupting your suit's functions. You have no radar, no communications, and no Repulsors when within range of the emitters' fields.

Spin the camera around to the right to find a marker in the distance. Fly toward the first emitter until you see the Turrets. Fire some Rockets at the Turrets and obliterate them before turning your attention on the Battlesuit and Soldiers. Once the area is clear, disable the emitter with a couple melee attacks. Refill your ammo next to the helipad with the Ammo Box. A Weapon Crate sits next to the big tower behind the helipad.

BASICS
ENEMIES
ARMOR
WEAPONS
UPGRADES
MISSIONS
UNLOCKABLES

## CONSERVE YOUR EXPLOSIVES

You don't have Repulsors with which to take out the Turrets, so you must demolish them with your Rockets or Missiles. Use the Ballistics gun on the Soldiers and save the explosives for the Turrets since they're more heavily armored and more difficult to destroy.

Look to the left to find another marker indicating the second emitter's location. Take out the Turrets mounted in front of the tower before disabling the emitter. Another Weapon Crate sits next to the helipad.

Continue around the perimeter to discover the third emitter. Destroy the Turrets with the suit's explosive weaponry before disabling the final emitter. Once the final emitter is rendered useless, you regain complete suit functionality. What a relief!

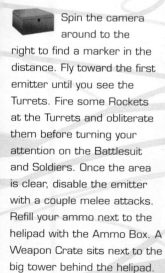

UNI BEAM:

003

REP BEAM:

675

## Disable the East Power Facility

You begin the mission facing to the North. So from there, turn to the right (facing East) and fly toward the waypoint. Use Afterburner Mode to cover the distance faster.

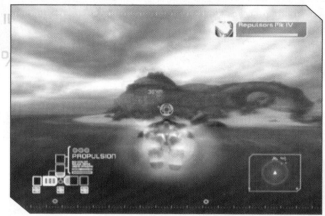

Upon reaching the island, take out the two Turrets ahead and continue on until you also crush the Tank down on the beach.

Look for a building marked with the number 23. There's

a Weapon Crate at its base. There's also an Ammo Box on a walkway located on the other side of the helipad. Proceed in the same direction to find yet another Weapon Crate.

Enter the facility and follow the path until you locate a couple of patrolling Battlesuits. Dodge in and out of the entryway and take them down with the Repulsors, using the doorframe as solid cover. Unleash melee attacks on the power station until it is completely demolished. However, watch out for the enemies as you exit the facility; they're not happy.

### RADAR JAMMING

**Each Power Facility has a radar jamming system nearby. Therefore, as you get closer, your suit will start to malfunction. Your first priority at each island should be to take that system out to get your radar back.**

Follow the path up the hill and eradicate the enemies ahead. The toughest of these are the two Battlesuits patrolling the grounds. The radar jamming system is just past the enemy squad, above the helipad.

### SHOTS FROM THE PROTON CANNON

**As the cannon begins to come online, huge blasts occasionally rain down on Iron Man—appearing as big, white columns. Keep moving to avoid getting hit. A single, direct hit causes Tony's heart to fail. However, the cannon must recharge after firing, so there is a short break between shots.**

SYS001
SYS002
SYS003
SYS004

SYS005
SYS006

BIO ACTIVE
VENT ACTI
RESP FLTR
OPTIC ACT

CYBERNET 2-4987-000-ARM
BOOT: 3845782372 OSU
290582394 -303

BASICS

ENEMIES

ARMOR

WEAPONS

UPGRADES

MISSIONS

UNLOCKABLES

## Disable the West Power Facility

Fly around the East island and take out the rest of the Turrets and any Helicopters that show up to reinforce the teams under fire. There are two more facilities that must be disabled. Fly toward the right (West) location next.

Turn to the right and head directly toward the power facility. You'll be forced to battle more Battlesuits and Turrets before destroying the radar jamming system.

Enter the facility and beat up the two Battlesuits with a few devastating melee attacks. With the enemy force wiped out, the next job is to destroy the power station itself! With this completed, head back outside and eliminate the enemies that have shown up to forestall any more of your progress.

## WATCH OUT FOR HELICOPTERS

As you travel between the islands, keep an eye on the radar for enemies flying toward you. Take down these Helicopters with Iron Man's Repulsors, but don't wait to watch their smoking husks fall into the water below—keep moving!

## Disable the North Power Facility

Fly to the final island and continue around the perimeter, taking out the Turrets along the way. Stop at the back of the island and fire a shot at the radar jamming system mounted atop a building. Once back at the front of the island, start picking off the enemies from a distance.

  Once you reach the island, light up the Turrets intended to provide a warm welcome and then direct your attention to the Battlesuits ahead. They're pulling out all the stops and they won't be as defeated easily. Destroy the Weapon Crate in the right corner and resupply at the Ammo Box in the other corner.

## STAY ON THE MOVE

As you hover and shoot at the enemy, be sure to keep moving from side to side to avoid getting hit with a shot from the Proton Cannon. There are just some AIM toys you don't play well with.

## The Proton Cannon is Exposed

Stay inside the doorway and pick off the Battlesuit that arrives outside. Exit the facility and fly back to the first island—the only remaining point on your radar.

Work your way towards the facility located in the back of this area, carefully taking out each enemy from a distance. A Weapon Crate is inside the destroyed wall on the left and another is located next to the crane on the right.

Drop down next to the cannon and hit it with some melee attacks to destroy this incredible threat. With the cannon in ruins, Bruno Horgan, a.k.a. Melter, emerges from inside the building. AIM has definitely raised the stakes...

SYS001    00 0098 2304112 151
SYS002    00 7802 1023401 674
SYS003    04 6730 3501313 012
SYS004    03 7345 2219313 512
SYS005    01 3462 2109867 990
SYS006    00 4403 1123406 003

EIO  ACTIVE
VENT  ACTI
RESP  FLTR
OPTIC  ACT

IIIIIIII    IIIIIIIII

Take out the Tank located in the doorway toward the back. Enter the facility at that entrance and go hand-to-hand with the Battlesuit inside. This final force was intended to keep you from destroying their final power station. Too bad. Let loose with some melee attacks to impress upon them the error of their ways. Disabling the final power station exposes the Proton Cannon.

# THE MELTER

**1** Horgan comes out firing with his pulse gun. Keep moving to avoid his fire. A roof has closed over the cannon, so you can't get too far away.

**2** Melter occasionally charges up his gun and fires a huge blast at you. If you see him charging, dash to hide on the other side of the destroyed cannon.

**3** Continue moving around the enclosed area, pelting Melter with Repulsor blasts, while you avoid his pulse shots. Take cover behind the cannon when he begins his charged attack and retaliate after avoiding the blast. After several shots, Horgan falls and you complete the mission.

..........32%
..........78%
..........78%

..........92%
..........88%
..........28%

..........12%
..........98%
..........46%

# 12 BATTLESUIT FACTORY

## MISSION DESCRIPTION

*AIM has been stealing your technology for years, and they're at it again. With a new factory in full production, AIM plans to build its own army of Battlesuits. It's time to put a stop to this.*

## MISSION OBJECTIVE

DESTROY THE BATTLESUIT FACTORY.

## COLLATERAL OBJECTIVES

INFILTRATE THE MILITARY BASE.

LOCATE THE SOURCE OF THE SIGNAL.

RECOVER STOLEN BLUEPRINTS.

INVESTIGATE THE PURPOSE OF THE FACILITY.

DESTROY AIM COMPUTER MAINFRAME.

## DEFAULT ARMOR

MARK I        MARK II        MARK III

## WEAPONS & AMMO

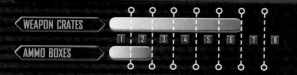

## ENEMIES

| | |
|---|---|
| BATTLESUITS | TANK |
| HELICOPTER | TURRETS |
| SOLDIERS | |

## Infiltrate the Military Base

You begin the mission directly in front of AIM headquarters. There's a Helicopter heading your way; blast it out of the sky and turn your attention onto the other threat at hand—Turrets. Destroy the four Turrets mounted around the entrance before moving in.

Drop to the platform below and approach the door. Follow the on-screen commands to open it and infiltrate the military base. A Tank, a Battlesuit, and a few Soldiers are there to bar your way. Eliminate them and destroy the Weapon Crate located in the front right corner.

Continue to the back of the room and blast the Soldier behind the desk on the left. Bash open the elevator on the right and drop to sub-floor 2.

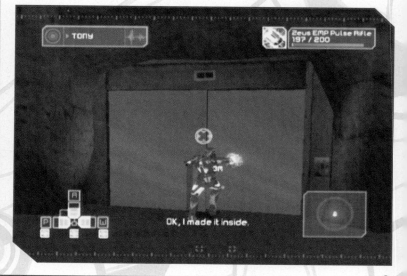

BASICS

ENEMIES

ARMOR

WEAPONS

UPGRADES

MISSIONS

UNLOCKABLES

Pick off the Soldier across the hall and demolish the Turret on the left. Shoot the computer sitting behind the counter to drop the security field. Watch out for the Soldiers and Battlesuit that arrive once the field is down. Eliminate them and then search around the corner until you find another elevator shaft. Use it to access sub-floor 3.

## *Locate the Source of the Signal*

Eliminate the Soldiers guarding the hallway and then run to the left into another room. Remain in the entry and pick off the Soldiers and destroy Turret inside. There's a vent on the right wall; bust it open and drop to sub-floor 4.

Look down to the lower level and pick off the Soldiers and Battlesuit from above. Eliminating the enemies from range during this mission is going to serve you well. Drop down, destroy the Weapon Crate on the right, and refill your ammunition from the Ammo Box on the walkway.

Exit the room through the door in the opposite corner. Run to the left and take out the Soldiers and Turret. This should lower the security field. Look back to see if it dropped and take a second to prepare yourself for the Battlesuit barreling down on your position.

Crush the Battlesuit and enter the room from which he emerged. The computer there should be destroyed to permanently drop the security field.

Follow the hallway and halt before you run into the three laser trip lines in your way—a new obstacle. Hover into the air and carefully fly over the lines. Continue hovering and head up along the ceiling to keep away from the laser lines. Destroy the door and escape into the next room.

A few Battlesuits and a Soldier have prepared a little welcome inside. Explain to them that they're foolish for standing against Iron Man, and destroy the Weapon Crate in the room before exiting out the door on the left.

A security field blocks the path to the right. Follow the hall and hover over the trip lines. Burst through the door to find the source of the signal! Take out the Soldiers inside.

## Recover Stolen Blueprints

Through the next door you find a couple Soldiers and Battlesuit. Security fields block two of the paths, and three trip lines block the third. There are two computers in the next room. Destroying the one to left disables the trip lines.

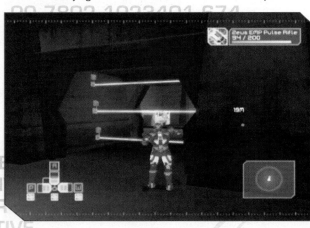

Enter the room and use the other computer to recover the blueprints. This also lowers the security field ahead, but two Battlesuits arrive to try to keep you from the areas instead. Obliterate them and demolish the computer in the next room to lower the security field in front of a nearby elevator shaft.

## Investigate the Purpose of the Facility

Dash back out into the hall, take out the Soldiers, and drop down to sub-floor 5. Two Battlesuits are standing on the other side of a hazardous electromagnetic area. Take out the Turret on the ceiling and then dodge behind the crates.

Remain on this side of the hazardous area and use the crates for cover while you whittle away at the Battlesuits' health. Pop up, launch a barrage of Rockets or Missiles and then duck back behind cover until they're defeated. Hover over the current and land next to the smoking scraps of the Battlesuits.

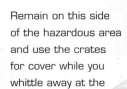

BASICS

ENEMIES

ARMOR

WEAPONS

UPGRADES

MISSIONS

UNLOCKABLES

Shoot out the glass directly in front of you and destroy the computer to lower the security field. Enter the next room and squash the Soldiers inside. In the back of the room, destroy the window and take out the two Turrets in the next area. Stand to the far right to get an angle on the left Turret.

Eliminate the other Soldiers in the room and drop to the lower level. Just under the spot where you entered the room sits a Weapon Crate. Destroy it before heading out the door on the other side of the room.

Through the next door and down the hall, you run into another electromagnetic area and three laser trip lines. Carefully hover between the trip lines and proceed through the next door into a shooting range.

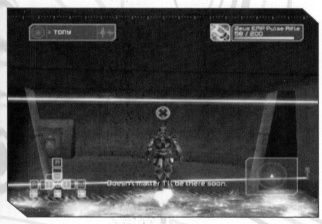

Follow the hall to find the room that you saw earlier. A big electromagnetic area with several trip lines makes for an extremely hazardous path. Hover into the air and carefully adjust your height as you pass between the trip lines. Watch out for the Soldiers that appear on the other side of the window.

Iron Man runs into four Battlesuits intent on stopping him here and now. Run to the far right side and take out one of the Battlesuits. Use the partial wall here as cover as you take out the remaining three. Once they're down, shoot out the glass that looks over the next room and the two Soldiers patrolling there. Refill your ammunition stores at the Ammo Box before proceeding through the next door or window.

## HOVERING UP AND DOWN

**Aim up or down slightly to adjust your height while hovering.**

A lone Battlesuit is waiting for you in the next room. Run up to it and take it down with some melee attacks. Go through the window and drop down to some tracks below.

The suit's Afterburner Mode comes online, so start screaming down the tracks. Two Turrets flank the door just ahead. Destroy them and then follow the commands to open the door.

Another Weapon Crate is directly in front of the group of three train engines. Two more Turrets are mounted on the ceiling guarding another door. Open the door and continue to fly down the tracks past more engines.

Again, take out the two Turrets and open another door. Fly down to the next engine, past a door on the right, and destroy the Weapon Crate. Head through this door and turn to the left.

### Destroy AIM Computer Mainframe

Through another opening is another electromagnetic area and trip lines. Carefully hover through the trip lines and destroy the computers in the next room. Watch out for the two Battlesuits that show up.

Hover back over the previous electromagnetic area and go through the door on the left to find some Tin Can Armor replicas.

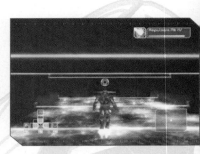

### Defeat Tin Can Armor Replicas

Press the switch on the left to release three of the Battlesuits. Either dodge their fire while taking them down with the Repulsors or run up to them and demolish them with some heavy melee strikes. Rest for a bit to allow the armor's self-repair processes to take effect, and then hit the second switch.

Again three Battlesuits swarm out to destroy their target—Iron Man. Destroy them and the press the third switch to fight the final three. Defeat them as you did the other two sets to complete the objective.

### Destroy the Main Emitter

Use the computer that is now marked on the radar to reveal the emitter in the middle of the room. Destroy it to complete the mission.

BASICS

ENEMIES

ARMOR

WEAPONS

UPGRADES

MISSIONS

UNLOCKABLES

# 13 SHOWDOWN

## MISSION DESCRIPTION

*Now mobile, but cornered, and armed with his own version of a mechanized suit, a dangerously armored Obadiah Stane threatens Pepper and the rest of the city. Return to Stark Industries and stop the desperation of the Iron Monger.*

## MISSION OBJECTIVE

BRING DOWN STANE.

## DEFAULT ARMOR

MARK I          MARK II          MARK III

## WEAPONS & AMMO

WEAPON CRATES

AMMO BOXES

| 1 | 2 | 3 | 4 | 5 | 6 | 7 | 8 |

## ENEMIES

OBADIAH "IRON MONGER" STANE

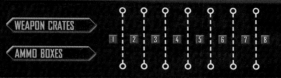

---

## IRON MONGER

**1** This is the final showdown with Obadiah Stane, also known as Iron Monger. The battle takes place in the street lined by automobiles.

**2** Occasionally, Stane will run back to the pile of cars at the end of the street, grab one, and hurl it at Iron Man. Hit him with a few missiles as he grabs the car, then be ready to dash out of the way.

**3** Stane fires a Gatling Gun and launches missiles at Iron Man when he isn't tossing cars. As he launches the missiles, dash from side to side to avoid them.

### MORE POWER TO ARMOR

If you get hit during his barrage of missiles, re-route the suit's power to Armor to survive the attack.

Boss Fight continued on next page >

# IRON MONGER

**4** If you get close to him, you can hit him with some melee attacks. But watch out, he will grab Iron Man and perform a bear hug. Follow the on screen commands to break free of his hold.

**5** Stay on the move to avoid the missiles and if he runs to your side of the street, fly over to his side. Continually launch missiles or use the Repulsor to eat away at Stane's health.

## EXPLOSIVE TANKER

Watch out for the blue tanker that sits at one end of the street. If it takes too much damage, it will explode, damaging you if you're close enough. Try to stay clear of it as you fight Stane.

**6** Once his health is down to about half, Stane flies to the top of a reactor where Pepper is being kept in the control center. An electrical current is being charged in the middle of this area. Once it is fully charged, it will short-circuit Stane's suit if he is caught in it.

**7** Hover around this electrified area trying to stay on the opposite side from Stane and unleash a continual barrage of Repulsor fire at him all the while. When fully charged, Stane gets hit with the strong electrical current. Continue this tactic, staying away from Stane, blasting away with the Repulsors, and allowing the current to take its toll on him. Stane can't stand forever and Iron Man will stand victorious before too long.

# UNLOCKABLES

BASICS

ENEMIES

ARMOR

WEAPONS

UPGRADES

MISSIONS

UNLOCKABLES

## ARMOR SELECTION

Iron Man's different armor suits are unlocked by completing certain missions. The suits you unlock on the PlayStation 2 and Wii consoles differ from the ones on the PSP. Refer to the following tables for when each is unlocked. After selecting a mission to play, you get the opportunity to pick the armor you wish to use.

| COMPLETE MISSION | SUIT UNLOCKED |
| --- | --- |
| 1: ESCAPE | MARK I |
| 2: FIRST FLIGHT | MARK II |
| 3: FIGHT BACK | MARK III |
| 6: FLYING FORTRESS | COMIC TIN CAN |
| 9: HOME FRONT | CLASSIC |
| 13: SHOWDOWN | SILVER CENTURION |

## CONCEPT ART

[Yo]u progress through the game and destroy the Weapon Crates, bonuses are [unlo]cked. You can find all of these in the Bonus menu once unlocked. Concept Art is [unlo]cked after finding certain numbers of Weapon Crates.

| CONCEPT ART UNLOCKED | NUMBER OF WEAPON CRATES FOUND |
| --- | --- |
| ENVIRONMENTS SET 1 | 6 |
| ENVIRONMENTS SET 2 | 12 |
| IRON MAN | 18 |
| ENVIRONMENTS SET 3 | 24 |
| ENEMIES | 30 |
| ENVIRONMENTS SET 4 | 36 |
| VILLAINS | 42 |
| VEHICLES | 48 |
| COVERS | 50 |

## VIDEOS

[Th]e following videos are available from the [be]ginning of the game in the Bonus menu.

[IRO]N MAN: TRAILER 1

[IRO]N MAN: TRAILER 2

[IRO]N MAN: UNMASKED

[HU]LK: THE BEAST WITHIN

[NE]XT AVENGERS

# IRON MAN

## OFFICIAL STRATEGY GUIDE

BradyGames Publishing
An Imprint of DK Publishing, Inc.
800 East 96th Street, 3rd Floor
Indianapolis, Indiana 46240

ISBN: 0-7440-1019-5

Printing Code: The rightmost double-digit number is the year of the book's printing; the rightmost single-digit number is the number of the book's printing. For example, 08-1 shows that the first printing of the book occurred in 2008.

11  10  09  08                                    4  3  2  1

Manufactured in the United States of America.

## BRADYGAMES STAFF

Publisher
**David Waybright**

Editor-In-Chief
**H. Leigh Davis**

Licensing Director
**Mike Degler**

Marketing Director
**Debby Neubauer**

International Translations
**Brian Saliba**

## CREDITS

Sr. Development Editor
**Christian Sumner**

Screenshot Editor
**Michael Owen**

Lead Designer
**Tim Amrhein**

Designer
**Dan Caparo**

Production Designer
**Bob Klunder**

## BRADYGAMES ACKNOWLEDGMENTS

A special thanks goes out to David Allen of SEGA who went beyond the call off duty to get this thing together in time. You rock! Thanks also to Dyna Lopez, Cindy Chau, Logan Parr, and Erica Mason.

## DAN BIRLEW'S ACKNOWLEDGMENTS

Dan Birlew would like to thank Leigh Davis for assigning me to this excellent project, and Christian Sumner for bringing me back into the fold and being an excellent project manager. Great thanks also to co-author Michael Owen for his technical help, and thanks to all the layout/design staff and marketing support at BradyGames. And thanks, as always, to my lovely wife Laura, for adhering to all the qualities which make her the perfect writer's wife.